W9-AZJ-167

# THE GOOD, THE BAD, AND THE UGLY
# CINCINNATI REDS

## HEART-POUNDING, JAW-DROPPING, AND GUT-WRENCHING
## MOMENTS FROM CINCINNATI REDS HISTORY

Mike Shannon

TRIUMPH
BOOKS

Triumph Books and colophon are registered trademarks of Random House, Inc.

Library of Congress Cataloging-in-Publication Data

Shannon, Mike.
    The good, the bad, and the ugly, Cincinnati Reds : heart-pounding, jaw-dropping, and gut-wrenching moments from Cincinnati Reds history / Mike Shannon.
      p. cm.
    Includes bibliographical references.
    ISBN-13: 978-1-60078-077-6
    ISBN-10: 1-60078-077-6
    1. Cincinnati Reds (Baseball team)—History. I. Title.
GV875.C65S53 2008
796.357'640977178—dc22

              2007051639

This book is available in quantity at special discounts for your group or organization. For further information, contact:

**Triumph Books**
542 South Dearborn Street
Suite 750
Chicago, Illinois 60605
(312) 939-3330
Fax (312) 663-3557

Printed in U.S.A.
ISBN: 978–1–60078–077–6
Design by Patricia Frey
Photos courtesy of AP/Wide World Photos unless otherwise indicated.

*For Jerry Hazelbaker, who grew up
loving the Cincinnati Reds.*

# CONTENTS

# FOREWORD

**W**hen Mr. Castellini approached me about managing the Cincinnati Reds, it took me about half a second to decide to accept the invitation. And why not? Managing a baseball team is what I do, and the Reds job is one you'd serve a 100-year apprenticeship in the bush leagues to get if you had to.

I've been in baseball a long time, and I've always been around greatness. When I was a youngster I had the honor of playing alongside the immortal Hank Aaron, who treated me like a kid brother and taught me how to be a major leaguer. In my prime, I played for the Los Angeles Dodgers, one of the greatest organizations in baseball history, and I participated in four League Championship Series and three World Series while wearing Dodger blue. As the skipper of the San Francisco Giants, and later the Chicago Cubs, I got to manage two of the game's biggest superstars, Barry Bonds and Sammy Sosa. And becoming manager of the Cincinnati Reds ranks right up there with all those other highlights in my career.

You see, no matter where I've been, there has always been a deep respect for the history and tradition represented by the Reds franchise. Heck, everybody knows that professional baseball was invented by the Reds! You add in the boys of 1919 that beat the Black Sox; Johnny Vander Meer; Ewell "the Whip" Blackwell; Big Klu; the youngest kid to play big-league ball, Joe Nuxhall; Chuck Harmon, one of the color-line-breaking pioneers; Frank Robinson and Vada Pinson; Pete Rose; Johnny Bench and all those other great players on the Big Red Machine; and so on and so on...man, you're talking about something I am proud to be a part of.

Baseball is a beautiful game to play and to watch, but at the major league level it's all about winning. The Reds organization believes that—I would never have signed on to lead this ballclub if it didn't. Mr. Castellini, Wayne Krivsky, and I are united in our efforts to bring back the glory days that Reds fans have relished so deeply in the past, and I believe that we will make it happen. Until that day when Fountain Square is jam-packed again with Cincinnati fans celebrating another world championship, Reds fans can relive many of the greatest, most spectacular, craziest, most poignant, and yes, even some of the most embarrassing moments in team history by reading this new book on the Reds. Author Mike Shannon did a fine job with it, as well he should have. After all, consider the great material he had to work with!

—Dusty Baker

# ACKNOWLEDGMENTS

The older I get, the longer the list of people I must thank when I reach the end of a book becomes. Now that this book on the Cincinnati Reds is finished, it is time for me to complete that most enjoyable task.

First of all, I'd like to thank Tom Bast of Triumph Books for the invite. Tom and I have known each other for years, but we've never gotten to work together until this book. I hope we get to do it again. I'd also like to thank Triumph's Adam Motin for his encouragement, enthusiasm, and flexibility.

The best place for an author to have friends is in a bookstore, and I am thankful for the friendship of the great Borders crew of Pam Branwart, Tony D'urso, Debbie Gibbons, Cory Highfield, Ray Muff, Tim Newkirk, Cassandra Rowland, and Cheryl Vagedes. They not only roll out the red carpet for me, but they also make their store an oasis for everybody who enters it.

In my spare time I currently work at the Greater Cincinnati and Northern Kentucky Airport for the greatest airline in the world, Comair. In any large company you expect to run into equal amounts of the good, the bad, and the ugly, but Comair is bursting with beautiful people, and I am truly thankful I get to work with the following: Bill Adams, Mike Barker, Stephen Bee, Dylan Beebe, Sabrina Bowers-Grant, Michele Buckley, Rachel Buntin, Lisa Caudill, Michael Clifton, Eric Coldiron, Marina Coors, Tom Dee, Michael DeJaco, Lat Diouf, Graeme Dorn, Jose Esteve, Tony Fegan,

Kae Lee Foster, Rochel Gomes, Paige Graham, Mark Graves, Sharon Graves, Rhonda Gregory, Allison Griffin, CarMarie Guzman-Maldonado, Christine Hays, Ryan Hazelrigg, Amber Heisel, Dorothy Abbey-Henderson, Lisa Henderson, Jen Hertensberg, Sarah Hipple, Connie Huber, Paula Hunterman, Phillippe Kontcho, Nellie Lonnemann, Waymond Mack, Mathleen Maipi, Michael McGreevy, Clark McMillen, Bill McNeeley, Phil Miazga, Sandy Morgan, Kiera O'Neill, Deb Pittman, Jen Pragar, Susan Ratz, Mariana Reichert, Robert Renfrow, Liz Rodriguez, Misty Rogers, Dorothy Ryan, Derrick Sanderson, Patti Schultz, Missy Sharp, Sharon Simpson, Delores Slover, Ahmad Smali, Farida Ulander, Paul Versteeg, Kim Vorhees, Tina Walden, Mike Walker, Nick Ward, Anthony Washington, Sean Webb, Pat Wegman, and Sharon Whiteley.

Although I have listed Greg Rhodes's fine books in the bibliography, Greg is due more than a perfunctory acknowledgment. Lee Allen has always been considered the dean of authors on the topic of the Cincinnati Reds, but in reality he surrendered that title to Greg long ago. Any author who writes about the Reds will find himself in debt to Mr. Rhodes, and I am no exception.

I also wish to thank the multitalented Bill McGill for so ably running *Spitball: The Literary Baseball Magazine;* Mark Schraf for continuing to bless me with his friendship; Mark Rea, managing editor of *Reds Report;* computer guru Keith Schneider; and my nephew Andrew Smiley, who will soon be in charge of the entire world, for building and maintaining the website mikeshannonbooks.com.

As always, I express my deepest gratitude and love to my incomparable mother and father, John and Willie Shannon; to my sisters and brothers (and their families): Sis, Susie, John, and Tim; to my beautiful wife Derms; and to our children, of whom we are so very proud: Megan, Casey, Mickey, Babe, and Nolan Ryan.

*Ad majorem Dei gloriam.*

# THE GOOD

Cincinnati is a conservative midwestern river town located on the mighty Ohio in the southwest corner of the Buckeye state, known for, as much as anything else, the game of baseball. In fact, it is difficult to think of Cincinnati without associating with it the city's most famous progeny, the Cincinnati Reds of the National League, who are direct descendants of the very first "base ballists" to ever play professionally. Oh, sure, the city has other claims to fame—including its delicious Skyline Chili, the mighty Procter & Gamble Company, and the Delta Queen paddle wheeler—but the conversation always comes around sooner or later to those red-and-white-clad boys of spring, summer, and (sometimes) fall, who give the city so much of its identity.

Like every city more than a few decades old, Cincinnati has seen its share of troubles. Its good citizens have endured disease, natural disasters, wars, economic downturns, and social unrest. Through it all the people have persevered, in large part because the Almighty programmed that sort of spirit into mankind, but also because the people of Cincinnati, as well as Reds fans everywhere, have had for almost a century and a half a ballteam of their own to follow religiously and to find comfort in. It is comforting that the Reds are there, playing almost daily in the spring and throughout the summer, and even when they fail to win the laurels, Reds fans stay loyal to the colors and the fellows because they know that if they can make it through the winter they will see the Reds begin again when the calendar brings a new season.

Like the Queen City itself, the Reds have had their ups and downs, their Good, their Bad, and their Ugly. Ask any Reds fan, though: they've had much more Good than anything else.

## YOU CAN'T DO BETTER THAN PERFECT!

The invention of baseball, like that of many other great things in this world, was for many years misattributed—to General Abner Doubleday, who had nothing whatsoever to do with the founding of the game. For his codifying of baseball's most elemental parameters and rules, Henry Chadwick is now recognized by historians as "The Father of Baseball," even as the search for the game's earliest precursors and appearances takes us further and further back in time. The most important thing about the game's early history that is not unknown or in dispute is the origin of professional baseball. Every American schoolchild knows, or should know, that the first baseball team in the world to play professionally was formed in Cincinnati, Ohio, in 1869, and that that team was known as the Cincinnati Red Stockings. That honor, my friend, is about as Good as it gets in baseball.

The honor is not merely academic—it means something to the fans, and players who pull on a Reds jersey feel a sense of pride and tradition that is inspired by few other teams. Reds players are also often quite demonstrative about revealing their pride in the franchise's heritage. I remember standing around the batting cage one day while the Reds were taking BP in Riverfront Stadium before a game with the San Francisco Giants. The Giants' general manager, Al Rosen, and his adolescent son were also standing nearby when Pete Rose stepped into the cage to hit. In between two of the line drives he was spraying all over the park, Rose turned toward Rosen's son and said with a big knowing grin, "How do you like being in Cincinnati, the birthplace of professional baseball?"

On the other hand, comedian George Carlin has asked, "If the Cincinnati Reds were the first professional baseball team, who did

# TOP 10 REDS NICKNAMES OF THE 19ᵗʰ CENTURY

1. "Icebox" Chamberlain (Elton P.)—Elton was a pitcher not easily rattled; he maintained his cool in the face of adversity.
2. "Buttercup" Dickerson (Lewis Pessano)—Dickerson, an outfielder, loved flowers.
3. "Bumpus" Jones (Charles Leander)—Jones's nickname was a corruption of bumpkin, as in "country bumpkin" or rube. He was from the small town of Cedarville, Ohio.
4. "Redleg" Snyder (Emanuel Sebastian)—the name was hung on Snyder in honor of his having been a member of the Cincinnati Redlegs team, who played in the National League in its first year of existence (1876). Even though Snyder played only that year for the Redlegs, the nickname stayed with him the rest of his career.
5. "White Wings" Tebeau (George E.)—the term referred to street cleaners or garbage workers of the era, and it is not clear why the moniker was hung on this outfielder who played for Cincinnati for three years (1887–1889).
6. "Cannonball" Crane (Edward Nicholas)—Crane was one of the fastest pitchers of the day. He also set the record for longest throw when he hurled a baseball more than 406 feet on October 12, 1884, in Cincinnati.
7. "Mother" Watson (Walter L.)—mother was a nickname for those who did not indulge in the typical ballplayer vices of smoking, drinking, swearing, or brawling. By all accounts, Watson conducted himself as a gentleman.
8. "Socks" Seybold (Ralph Orlando)—not a reference to footwear, but socks as in striking the ball forcefully, which Seybold could do. The outfielder led the American League in home runs with 16 in 1902.
9. "Silver" King (Charles Frederick)—a reference to the pitcher's prematurely gray hair.
10. "Cherokee" Fisher (William Charles)—a reference to the pitcher's Cherokee Indian ancestry. Not a particularly clever nickname but one that sounds great.

they play?" Carlin's joke hinges on the zanily logical assumption that since pro teams play pro teams today, whoever the Red Stockings played in that initial contest of the 1869 season must have been a professional team, too, thus making Cincinnati's opponent an equally "first" professional team!

Carlin obviously was not trying to dis the Red Stockings; he just wanted to make a funny. All joking aside, though, Carlin raises an interesting point, which many fans have not thought about. Who did the Red Stockings play? Other pro teams or amateur teams? If they only played amateur teams, what was the big deal about them winning all the time? And what league were they in?

To begin with, at the time there were no leagues for the Red Stockings to join, as the first professional baseball league, the National Association, was not formed until 1871. All teams were amateur and independent, which means they made their schedules themselves, usually on a home-and-away two-game basis with other clubs. Furthermore, the Red Stockings were the first overtly professional team that paid every player on the club a salary and then expected the players to take their participation seriously in all respects, as if playing ball were their job. Finally, as Greg Rhodes and John Erardi have pointed out in their wonderful book, *The First Boys of Summer*, the Red Stockings did play some strictly amateur outfits in 1869, who were invariably overwhelmed, but the top clubs that went up against the Red Stockings had their own professionals in uniform. The difference was that the Red Stockings' opponents did not pay all their players, nor did they pay them openly. The Red Stockings in essence took an occupation that was being practiced partially and in secret and transformed it into a legitimate and public profession.

The Red Stockings also proved the superiority of professional teams over amateur ones. This is something we take for granted, but in 1869 the concept was not the truism it is today. Once the 1869 Red Stockings got off to their fast start and began to gain a national reputation, the best clubs in the country, all technically amateur ones, looked forward to challenging, and defeating, these

**The 1869 Cincinnati Red Stockings are generally acknowledged to be the first professional baseball team.** (Photo courtesy of Getty Images.)

new professionals, the Cincinnati Base Ball Club (as the Red Stockings were officially called).

Led by former cricket pros Harry and George Wright, the Red Stockings opened their 1869 season in Cincinnati with a 45–9 victory over another local club, the Great Westerns. The date of the game, little remembered even in Cincinnati, was May 4, 1869. On May 31 the team embarked on a monthlong tour of the East that would thrust them into the national sporting spotlight and send the baseball fans of Cincinnati into a rooting frenzy. The Red Stockings went 20–0 on the road trip, defeating a number of well-known top clubs, including the Troy (NY) Haymakers, Harvard College, New York Mutuals, Brooklyn Atlantics, New York Eckfords, Philadelphia Atlantics, Washington Nationals, and National Olympics. Back in Cincinnati on July 1 the Red Stockings were hailed as heroes. They enjoyed a parade and a luncheon in their honor, and after easily winning an exhibition match they were awarded a 28-foot-long trophy bat, inscribed with their names. On July 25, the team's winning streak reached 30 games—barely. It took a three-run rally in the bottom of the ninth to defeat the Forest Citys of Rockford, Illinois, 15–14.

The Red Stockings became so famous so quickly that they were invited to California to play. With their record standing at 43–0, the team made the unprecedented "Western trip," demolishing the inferior competition they faced on the way there and back—the average score in their six games against San Franciscan teams was 56–6. Playing their final game at home in a rematch on November 7, the Red Stockings beat the Mutuals of New York 17–8 to finish 57–0.

The perfect season of 1869 ensured the fame of the Red Stockings, and it ushered in the dawn of professional baseball. The one thing it did not do was ensure the existence of the Red Stockings. The Red Stockings continued their perfect ballplaying into 1870 and acquired an image of invincibility, but the winning streak could not last forever. It came to an end on June 15 after reaching 81 games. The Red Stockings lost in New York to the Atlantics in extra innings, 8–7. Club president Aaron Champion was crushed by the loss and sent a telegram back to Cincinnati that would become famous:

The finest game ever played. Our boys did nobly, but fortune was against us. Eleven innings played. Though beaten, not disgraced.

In reality, the Red Stockings were done in by their poor fielding. It wouldn't be the team's only loss in 1870 either, as the Red Stockings finished their second season with a 67–6 record. Despite the fact that this record made for the best winning percentage in the country, the Mutuals and not the Red Stockings were considered the champions of baseball for 1870, because of the prevalent screwy system for determining the champion.

# LINEUP OF THE 1869 RED STOCKINGS

Most serious Reds fans can name the most frequent starting lineups of Reds championship teams, if not the entire rosters. They are probably less familiar with the lineup of the 1869 Red Stockings, but as the first professional baseball team ever, the Red Stockings deserve to be remembered. Plus they had only 10 players on the roster. When you refer to the Red Stockings nine, you've just about included everybody! Here are the 10 immortals of '69.

| Player | Age | Position | Salary for 1869 | Off-Season Occupation |
|--------|-----|----------|-----------------|------------------------|
| Charlie Gould | 21 | 1B | $800* | bookkeeper |
| Charles Sweasy | 21 | 2B | $800 | hatter |
| Fred Waterman | 23 | 3B | $1,000 | bookkeeper |
| George Wright | 22 | SS | $1,800 | engraver |
| Andy Leonard | 22 | LF | $800 | hatter |
| Harry Wright | 34 | CF | $2,000 | jeweler |
| Cal McVey | 18 | RF | $800 | piano maker |
| Doug Allison | 22 | C | $800 | marble cutter |
| Asa Brainard | 27 | P | $1,100 | insurance broker |
| Richard Hurley | 21 | SUB | $600 | |
| Oak Taylor | # | SUB | | |

* Different sources offer conflicting amounts, and these salaries are the ones likely to be the most accurate in the opinion of *The First Boys of Summer* authors Rhodes and Erardi.

# Oak Taylor was a substitute for regular substitute Hurley on the Red Stockings Western tour during the second half of the 1869 season. Little about him is known.

Just as astonishing as the 1869 perfect season and the 81-game winning streak was the demise of the club—the Red Stockings disbanded after 1870. The club never did attain the profitability that the directors had hoped for; fan support had dwindled; and some of the players (particularly second baseman Charlie Sweasy) had sullied the image of the club with ungentlemanly behavior. Worst of all, the Red Stockings were driven out of business by their own success. The market for top ballplaying talent escalated overnight, and the

# FAST FACTS

Harry and George Wright are the two most famous and important brothers to play for the Reds. They were members of the original Red Stockings team that went undefeated in 1869. Shortstop George was the best player on the team, while older brother Harry was the captain, center fielder, and relief pitcher.

**George Wright, along with his brother Harry, were two of the stars of the Red Stockings' undefeated team in 1869.**
(Photo courtesy of Getty Images.)

Cincinnati Base Ball Club felt that paying the salaries it would take to retain its players would push the club into bankruptcy. Thus the first professional baseball team in history and the only one to ever complete a perfect season brought about but did not join the first professional league in baseball history, the National Association of Professional Base Ball Players (the NAPBBP), which was formed in 1871. Professional baseball returned to its birthplace five years later, when the Red Stockings joined a new league, the National, in 1876. There have been no more perfect seasons in the Queen City since 1869, just a perfect match between a team and its legions of adoring fans that has its origin in the famous Red Stockings of '69.

## MORE FIRSTS AND INNOVATIONS

Because the Red Stockings were the first professional team, Cincinnati established a number of other, collateral firsts. For instance, under the leadership of manager Harry Wright, the Red

Stockings were the first team to hold regular, organized practices that included drills designed to inculcate the fundamentals. The club was the first professional team to sign players to contracts calling for specific, predetermined salaries; the first to wear knickers and colored (red) baseball stockings; the first to pull off a triple play (on August 4 against the Central Citys of Syracuse); the first, and probably the last, to play a game with eight players (nevertheless, Cincinnati defeated the Kentuckys 58–9 on November 3 in Louisville); and the first to play games on both coasts of the country. In addition, the term "ace," meaning a team's best pitcher, came into use as a derivative of the first name of the Red Stockings' undefeated pitcher of 1869, Asa Brainard. And the first glove was used by Red Stockings catcher Doug Allison, who cut the fingers off of a winter mitten and used it to protect his sore left palm from the hard pitches of Mr. Brainard.

All of these firsts and innovations (and many more) accomplished by the Red Stockings were just the beginning, as once in motion Cincinnati kept the momentum going and continued to be a pacesetter for the game of baseball.

In 1877, when the Reds were members of the first National League, one of their outfielders, Bob Addy, became the first player to steal a base by sliding into it. Pitcher Will White, the winningest pitcher in team history, was the first professional player to wear glasses during competition. When Deacon White, Will's older brother, became the Reds' catcher in 1878, the Reds fielded the first brother battery in history; and sometime in 1880 Reds catcher Buck Ewing became the first backstop to assume a squatting position behind the batter.

The firsts and innovations continued when the Reds played in the American Association from 1882 through 1889. The Reds were the driving force in the formation of the AA after being kicked out of the National League for their insistence on selling beer in their ballpark. The American Association, which allowed the sale of beer as well as games on Sunday, became known as "The Beer and Whiskey League." The Reds won the new league's first championship in 1882, which would be Cincinnati's only pennant-winning season until 1919. The club's 1882 record of

# AN ELECTRIC EVENING

The Reds were the first major league franchise to host an official game played under the lights. The game took place on May 24, 1935, at Crosley Field, and chief among the pomp and circumstance attending the game was the gimmick of having the 632 lights turned on at dusk when President Franklin Roosevelt pushed a button at the White House. The crowd roared with excitement to see Crosley Field lit up like the family parlor, and the game began after the Reds and Phillies were given 15 minutes to grow accustomed to the artificial illumination. Paul Derringer held the Phillies to six hits in a 2–1 Reds win, and the success of the game guaranteed that night baseball was here to stay, even though the rest of Major League Baseball was slow to embrace the innovation.

55–25 is still the highest winning percentage (.688) in team history. Team president Aaron Stern introduced two baseball innovations during this time, one kooky and one elemental but still ahead of its time. In 1882, Stern sought to brighten up the diamond by having each of his players wear a different colored uniform. Bad idea, quickly abandoned. A year later Stern put numbers on the backs of Reds uniforms,  but the players, noting that prison inmates wore numbers, objected and convinced Stern to discontinue the experiment.

The Reds claimed the game's first ambidextrous pitcher when Tony Mullane retired Pittsburgh's Tom Brown on a left-handed pitch after getting two strikes on Brown with right-handed pitches, and Cincinnati sportswriter Ren Mulford introduced the terms "hot corner" and "fan" (from fanatic) into the baseball lexicon.

The most significant innovation of the Reds' American Association days happened after the conclusion of the 1882 regular season, when they invited the National League champion Chicago club to play a two-game exhibition series in Cincinnati. Chicago accepted the invitation, and the two teams split the series, the Reds winning the first game 4–0, Chicago the second

2–0. The pair of exhibition games between league champions was not the first World Series, as the two teams refused to play a rubber match despite the pleas of fans in both cities for them to do so. Yet it was definitely the precursor to the first World Series, which were staged between the two leagues beginning in 1884.

Even after they rejoined the National League in 1890—the league in which they have played ever since—the Reds pulled more innovations and firsts out of their sleeves. The Reds introduced the submarine pitching delivery, dugouts (actually awnings), the team trainer, shin guards for catchers, the bottle bat, dragging the infield during a game, air travel, the hitters' background, the practice of posting an "E" on the scoreboard to indicate a fielding error, night baseball, air-conditioned press boxes and dugouts, and the all-synthetic infield. And these are merely the major innovations the Reds intentionally introduced. In many other instances either the Reds were one of the parties involved in a baseball first (the installation of the screen on the foul pole) or a baseball innovation came about because of the actions of a Reds player (umpires' hand signals, for instance).

Of course, Reds players, both as individuals and as a team, have been the first to accomplish many playing feats. Two of the greatest of these feats involved pitching performances that will likely never be repeated. The first came on May 2, 1917, when the Reds' Fred Toney hooked up with the Chicago Cubs' James "Hippo" Vaughn in the ultimate pitching duel, a game during which the pitchers on both teams pitched no-hitters! During the first nine innings only two men reached base against Toney, both via the free pass. Three batters reached against Hippo Vaughn—

## FAST FACTS

The Reds' first world championship of the modern era came in 1919, when the Reds beat the Chicago White Stockings. Accused of losing the Series on purpose in a gambling scandal, that Chicago team became known thereafter as the "Black Sox."

# THE 1969 ALL-TIME REDS TEAM

To commemorate the 100th anniversary of professional baseball and the birth of the 1869 Cincinnati Red Stockings, fans were asked to pick an all-time Reds team. Here is the way the 1969 voting went. The most unfamiliar name on this team for most fans today is that of Hughie Critz, who played six-plus years for the Reds. An outstanding fielder who led the National League four times in fielding percentage, Critz batted .322 in his rookie year and .280 overall for the Reds.

First base: Ted Kluszewski
Second base: Hughie Critz
Shortstop: Roy McMillan
Third base: Heinie Groh
Right field: Frank Robinson
Center field: Edd Roush
Left field: Pete Rose
Catcher: Ernie Lombardi
Right-handed pitcher: Bucky Walters
Left-handed pitcher: Eppa Rixey

two by walks and a third on an error—but Vaughn wound up facing the minimum as the first two runners were erased in double plays and the third when he was caught stealing. As the ninth inning of this historic game ended, the fans at Chicago's Weeghman Park delivered a standing ovation intended to salute both pitchers. The Reds quickly brought the fans and the game back down to earth, scoring in the top of the tenth on hits by Larry Kopf and Jim Thorpe sandwiched around an error. Ironically, it was the first run the Reds had scored in 35 innings. Toney then set the Cubs down 1–2–3 to finish the game with his no-hitter intact, but not before receiving a scare. The closest thing to a Cubs hit came with one out in the bottom of the tenth when Fred Merkle hit a drive into deep left field. It appeared as if the ball was headed for the bleachers, but at the last moment Reds left fielder Manuel Cueto reached up and speared it over his head at the wall.

While it remains the only double no-hit game in major league history, Toney's feat depended in part on the opposing team's pitcher. Johnny Vander Meer pulled off his most stellar pitching achievement all by himself; becoming the first and to-date the only major league pitcher to throw consecutive no-hitters. Vander Meer's first no-hitter came at home (in front of only 10,311 fans) on June 11, 1938, against the Boston Bees. Vandy walked three, but the excellent control he had over his curveball made his fastball look twice as fast, and the Boston hitters really didn't have a chance. In the ninth inning Boston manager Casey Stengel sent three consecutive pinch-hitters up to the plate in an effort to break the spell, but Vander Meer mowed them down. Vander Meer's next start came on June 15 at Ebbets Field in Brooklyn where a sellout crowd showed up to watch him and the first night game in Dodgers history—another 15,000 fans had to be turned away by the fire department. If ever a baseball player rose to the occasion, it was Vander Meer, who twirled another no-hitter, despite walking eight batters. As if he had intentionally decided to maximize the tension, Vander Meer retired the leadoff batter in the bottom of the ninth inning and then proceeded to walk the bases loaded! After Reds manager Bill McKechnie came out to calm him down, Vandy induced Dodger center fielder Ernie Koy to ground out, third to home, for the second out. Shortstop Leo Durocher was the next hitter, and when Harry Craft squeezed the soft fly ball that Leo lofted into center field, it was over. Vander Meer's next start came in Boston in front of another sellout crowd anxious to see if the Reds' sudden star could pull off the unthinkable. After walking the game's leadoff batter, Vandy retired 10 in

## FAST FACTS

The first official night game in major league history was played on May 24, 1935, at Crosley Field. The Reds beat the Philadelphia Phillies 2–1.

a row, but that was as far as he got, as a Deb Garms single in the fourth inning ended the streak of hitless innings. Still, it was an amazing run. The Reds won the game 14–1 with Vander Meer surrendering only three hits. With his 21 consecutive hitless innings pitched, Vander Meer was unable to match Cy Young, who had set the record in 1904 with 23, but he set a club record for consecutive scoreless innings with 32 and a major league record for fewest hits allowed (3) in three consecutive games.

**Johnny Vander Meer threw back-to-back no-hitters for the Reds in 1938, still the only major leaguer to accomplish such a feat.** (Photo courtesy of Getty Images.)

# HOME ADDRESSES

The history of Reds ballparks is as fascinating as that of the team itself, and from the beginning of the franchise Reds players and fans have lived by the saying, "There's no place like home."

The first ballpark in Reds history was the Union Grounds, where the 1869 Red Stockings played their home matches. Like all early ballparks the Union Grounds was built of wood, and its main structure was a large covered grandstand behind home plate floridly called "The Grand Duchess." After the third-base stands were double-decked in 1870, the park seated about 4,000. The Union Grounds was located roughly where the Cincinnati Union Terminal sits about a mile and a half from downtown, and though its playing dimensions have never been discovered, we do know that no one ever hit a home run over its fences. When the Reds joined the National League in 1876 they moved into a recently built ballpark located near Spring Grove Avenue and the Mill Creek about four miles from downtown. With its oblong shape, the Avenue Grounds was very deep in left and center and so shallow in right that a very high wall, a "Red Monster" so to speak, was erected there in an effort to keep the baseballs from flying out of the park. In 1880 the Reds moved to yet another new ballpark, the Bank Street Grounds, since it was a mile closer to downtown. Interestingly, the Bank Street Grounds also hosted circuses and Wild West shows, making it a multipurpose facility, just like Riverfront Stadium would be a century later. True to form, the Reds introduced another ballpark innovation at the Bank Street Grounds: the posting of players' names and up-to-date scores of other games (received via telegraph) on the ballpark's scoreboard.

The Reds lost their lease on the Bank Street Grounds after the 1883 season to a team in the upstart Union Association and had to scramble to find new lodgings. Team president Aaron Stern selected the land at Findlay and Western Avenues, the site of an abandoned brickyard, and this plot became the sacred ground where Reds ballparks would stand for the next 86 years, from 1884 to June 24, 1970.

At first the new park built of wood and iron by the Reds had no official name. It was sometimes called "American Park" after the league the Reds played in, the American Association, and it made a most inauspicious debut. After the first game on May 1, 1884, an entrance ramp collapsed, injuring several fans. The *Cincinnati Enquirer,* which supported the new Union Association team, exaggerated the extent of the injuries and even claimed that a fan was killed, but as author Greg Rhodes has pointed out, no deaths occurred. The Reds paid the medical bills of the injured fans and added entrance ramps to ease the flow of traffic into and out of the ballpark. When the Reds rejoined the National League in 1890, "American Park" became known as "League Park." Early in the 1900 season League Park caught fire in the wee hours of the morning. The entire park burned down except for a 50-foot section of the covered pavilion in right field. The Reds had to play seven home games on the road while a new grandstand was built. The team also took this opportunity to relocate the diamond, something that happened several times in the coming years. In 1902 a lavish new grandstand was built in time for the opening of the season. Known today as the "Palace of the Fans," this new grandstand featured classical columns, pillars, and other architectural flourishes reminiscent of the architecture that had been displayed at the Chicago World's Fair in 1892. Reds owner John T. Brush, a department store magnate, catered to the upper classes by installing 19 luxury boxes in the top level of the grandstand and to the lower classes by providing them with cheap seats at field level, called "Rooters' Row," where beer and whiskey were readily available for purchase. The crowning touch of the new edifice was a centrally situated cornice which proudly bore the city's name, just in case somebody didn't know whom to credit for such a grand structure.

By 1911 the populace of Cincinnati had become disenchanted with the Palace of the Fans. It was simply too small to accommodate large crowds, and the many columns and pillars, while pretty, obstructed the view. The low ceiling of Rooters' Row also made it impossible for patrons there to follow the flight of fly balls. Cincinnati needed a new ballpark, so club president Garry Herrmann commissioned a local firm to design and build one. The new ballpark, which opened on April 11, 1912,

# TOP 10 NATIVE SONS: THE BEST REDS PLAYERS BORN IN CINCINNATI (BASED ON THEIR PERFORMANCES AS REDS PLAYERS)

Cincinnati has always been a hotbed of baseball talent. Hundreds of Cincinnati kids have grown up to be major league players, and the Reds love to have native sons on the roster. Nobody but the Reds would even give Pete Rose a look out of high school, and as the story goes the only reason the Reds gave Rose a tryout was as a personal favor to his uncle, who was a bird dog for the club. Having roots in Cincinnati is one of the main reasons that players like Rose, Larkin, Parker, and Oester have been such fan favorites.

- Pete Rose—all-time hit king.
- Barry Larkin—19-year career, all with Reds. Future Hall of Fame shortstop.
- Dave Parker—694 hits, 107 HR. Led league in doubles and RBIs in 1985.
- John "Long John" Reilly—10-year career, all with Reds. 1,352 hits. Led league one time in triples, HR, and RBIs.
- Jim Brosnan—valuable bullpen member of 1961 pennant winner. 29 wins, 43 saves in Reds career.
- Ron Oester—13-year career, all with Reds. 1,118 hits.
- Miller Huggins—Hall of Fame manager with Yankees, was first a scrappy second baseman for Reds. 734 hits in six seasons.
- Ethan Allen—outfielder for Reds (1926–1930), 425 hits.
- Charlie Gould—first baseman and only native son on 1869 Red Stockings.
- Herm Wehmeier—wild left-handed pitcher, earned 49 of 92 career wins as a Red.

featured a double-decked grandstand running from first to third base. Single-deck pavilions extended down both foul lines to the outfield walls, and a bleacher section stood in the right-field corner. Herrmann named the new park Redland Field, a nickname sometimes used for League Park, and it was the first concrete and steel ballpark ever built by the Reds. The name Redland Field would last until 1934 when the ballyard was rechristened Crosley Field in honor of team owner Powel Crosley.

The original outfield distances at Redland Field were quite lengthy—393 feet to right field, 415 to center, and 348 to left—but these distances were later shortened several times, as the ballpark went through a dizzying array of changes and modifications over the years. While not the most beautiful ballpark ever built, Redland/Crosley had many unique features that endeared it to Reds fans, including the Superior Towel and Linen Service laundry and the Burger Beer sign atop the laundry, which loomed over the left-field wall for a time; the left-field "terrace" or steep incline, which often caused opposing outfielders to stumble when they had to go back to the wall for a fly ball; the "Goat Run" additional seating section in front of the right-field bleachers; and the massive 58-foot-tall scoreboard, with its famous Longines clock sandwiched between advertisements, that was erected in left-center field in 1957.

Crosley Field was the only Cincinnati ballpark that generations of Reds fans knew, and many memorable events took place there, such as four World Series (1919, 1939, 1940, and 1961) and two All-Star Games (1938 and 1953); the appearance of the youngest player in modern baseball history when 15-year-old Joe Nuxhall pitched ⅔ of an inning in 1944; Ewell Blackwell's club-record 16th win in a row (1947); Walker Cooper's club-record 10 RBIs and 15 total bases in one game (1949); an NL record-tying 221 home runs hit by the 1956 Reds; the longest game in club history, a 21-inning 1–0 loss to the San Francisco Giants in 1967; and no-hitters thrown by Hod Eller (1919), Johnny Vander Meer (1938), Clyde Shoun (1944), Ewell Blackwell (1947), and Jim Maloney (1969) for the Reds and Tex Carleton (Brooklyn, 1940), Lon Warneke (St. Louis, 1942), and Don Wilson (Houston, 1969) against the Reds.

Crosley Field finally began to outlive its usefulness in the 1960s. The seating capacity of the park was no longer adequate; the neighborhood that had given the ballpark much of its urban character had begun to deteriorate; and the parking situation, which had always been a problem, became untenable. Crosley was replaced by a state-of-art, multipurpose sports arena called Riverfront Stadium, which opened in mid-1970. Riverfront was part of a stadium building boom in America, just as Redland/Crosley Field had been, and critics complained that its circular shape and artificial surface made it indistinguishable from similar new stadiums in Atlanta, Philadelphia, Pittsburgh, and St. Louis. Such criticism overlooked the considerable virtues of the place. Fans loved its location, which made it easily accessible by two major highways, and the three-level garage beneath the stadium provided plenty of parking. Riverfront was also convenient to downtown, and its construction sparked a revival of much of the rest of the adjacent areas. There were no columns or pillars inside to obstruct the views, and the columnar design of the stadium's outer shell was classic. The seating capacity was enlarged by almost 40 percent over Crosley Field; the artificial turf made rain-outs almost nonexistent (an important consideration for the many Reds fans who came to games from out of town); the stadium was easy to keep clean and easy to get into and out of; and the Reds were able to keep ticket prices there as low as could be found in the major leagues. Riverfront Stadium sat on Cincinnati's doorstep, and it became a visual symbol of the city itself. Best of all, the Reds were able in the 1970s to mold their team to take advantage of the skills that Riverfront as a playing arena rewarded: speed, great defense, and power hitting. No finer tribute to Riverfront Stadium could be made than to say that it was "The Home of the Big Red Machine."

Unfortunately for fans who had grown accustomed to Riverfront Stadium, the economic situation in baseball in the late 1990s mandated that the Reds move to a new ballpark that would generate extra revenue through the sale of luxury boxes, which Riverfront could not accommodate. While the Reds played one final season in Riverfront in 2002, its replacement, the Great American Ball Park, was constructed right next door. No expense was spared in the design and construction of GAB, which came in at $280 million, compared to $45 million for Riverfront Stadium.

**The Reds hosted the Atlanta Braves in the first game ever played in Cincinnati's Riverfront Stadium.**

Better sight lines from almost every seat in the house, a stunning view of the Ohio River and Northern Kentucky from any of the upper deck seats, and the Reds Hall of Fame, which was completed a year and a half after the ballpark opened, were all improvements in favor of the Great American Ball Park. But what really made the fans fall in love with GAB at first sight were all the historical elements that the designers and architects crammed into the place. Everywhere you turn in GAB you run into something that hearkens back to the rich history and tradition of the Queen City and the Cincinnati Reds: the huge "Spirit of Baseball" limestone relief that adorns the west end of the Reds administration building at the entrance to the ballpark courtyard; life-size bronze statues of Ernie Lombardi, Ted Kluszewski, Joe Nuxhall, and Frank Robinson that stand in the mock infield that covers the courtyard; two beautiful, mural-size team mosaics of Italian marble, one depicting the members of the 1869 Red Stockings and the other the "Great Eight" members of the Big Red Machine; a massive photographic mural of Pete Rose's 4,192 bat and ball attached to the back of the scoreboard and visible to those outside the park; a replica of the Crosley Field Longines clock, which sits atop the main scoreboard above the left-field bleachers; "famous dates in Reds history" banners, which line the Second Street sidewalk next to the ballpark; a band of famous Reds quotations printed on the walls all the way around the ballpark on the suite level; retired uniform numbers that hang on the facade underneath the press box; Joe Nuxhall's famous radio sign-off ("Rounding third and heading for home") in neon on the northern face of the team administration building; and the riverboat-reminiscent Pepsi Power Stacks in the right-center-field bleachers that emit fireworks for home runs by Reds batters and smoke for strikeouts by Reds pitchers. Great American Ball Park still sparkles with a sense of freshness and novelty, but the verdict on it has already been turned in. While it is surely a scenic and comfortable place to watch a ballgame, GAB has also become in a very short time the living and breathing embodiment of the love affair that has existed for a century and a half between the Cincinnati Reds and their diehard fans.

## THE REDS HALL OF FAME

Reds fans are lucky that they have an official Hall of Fame that recognizes the contributions of the best players to their favorite team. Not all teams have such an institution. And the Reds Hall of Fame, the largest and oldest team Hall of Fame in existence, is one of those wonderful perks that make being a Reds fan such a good thing.

The Reds Hall of Fame wasn't always as good as it is today. It began as a cooperative venture between the Reds and the Cincinnati Chamber of Commerce, and the first election, a fan vote, was held in 1958. The first ballot contained 25 names and was heavily freighted with recently retired players, so it's no surprise

# THE GOOD PETE

For good or for bad, Pete Rose remains the face of the Cincinnati Reds franchise. His greatness as a player has never been in question, despite all his troubles, his banishment from baseball, and his ineligibility for Cooperstown. He remains the most beloved player to ever wear a Reds uniform, and even those who have written him off as a sad incorrigible respect his accomplishments on the diamond. The Reds organization has not forgotten Rose either. Even though Rose is not an official member of the Reds Hall of Fame, its most impressive permanent display is one which pays tribute to him: the huge pile of baseballs stacked up behind a glass wall in the southern stairwell, one baseball for each of his 4,256 major league hits. In 2007 the Reds also ran a 2,500 square-foot memorabilia and artifact exhibition dedicated to Rose called "Pete: The Exhibit." The bloom will never fade off the Rose celebrated in that exhibit, and to remind Reds fans of just how great a

Despite Rose's transgressions, the Reds Hall of Fame hosted a Pete Rose exhibit in 2007 that featured the bat Pete used to notch hit 4,192.

player Pete Rose was, the *Cincinnati Enquirer* published in its coverage of the Rose exhibition the following list of Rose's major records:

- Most career hits: 4,256
- Most hits by a switch-hitter: 4,256
- Most total bases by a switch-hitter: 5,752
- Most games played: 3,562
- Most winning games played: 1,972
- Most at-bats: 14,053
- Most singles: 3,215
- Most seasons of 200+ hits: 10
- Most seasons of 600+ at-bats: 17
- Most seasons of 150+ games: 17
- Only player to play 500+ games at five different positions: first base (939); left field (671), third base (634), second base (628), right field (595)
- Highest fielding percentage by an outfielder, 1,000+ games: .991
- NL record for most career runs: 2,165
- NL record for most career doubles: 746
- NL record for most games with five or more hits: 10
- Modern NL record for longest consecutive game hitting streak: 44
- Modern NL record for most consecutive game hitting streaks of 20 or more games: 7

that the five players elected were all members of the 1940 world championship team: Paul Derringer, Ernie Lombardi, Frank McCormick, Johnny Vander Meer, and Bucky Walters. All five members of this first class showed up at Crosley Field on July 18, 1958, to participate in the induction ceremonies prior to the doubleheader between the Reds and Cardinals.

This was a good start, but the entire enterprise was plagued by poor planning and methodology. For one thing, the stated eligibility standard was far too low. All that was required for eligibility was that a player be retired and have played at least three years with the Reds. Such a low standard practically guaranteed that some unqualified players would be put on the ballot. Second, the skewed first ballot indicated that the committee responsible for producing it was not up to the task of conducting a fair and thorough review of all eras of Reds history. And finally, the rules governing election were not clear as to whether election required a certain number of votes, a certain percentage of votes, or a certain ranking (such as the top two or three) among all players receiving votes.

Somehow, despite these problems, the process went on, and new members were elected every year. From 1959 through 1968, at least two (and as many as six) new members were elected each season. From 1969 through 1984, the process was apparently streamlined to admit only one new member each year. And then in 1984 there was no election at all. Marge Schott had taken over the ballclub, and she saw no value in the concept of a Reds Hall of Fame, only the costs of paying for the plaques and the traveling expenses of the new inductees. Jon Braude, the Reds publicity director at the time, did recognize the value of the Reds Hall of Fame, and he managed to keep the elections going for three more years (despite Schott's lack of support). But then, in 1989, stymied by a lack of interest in the elections on the part of the Cincinnati media and flummoxed by an attempt to get catcher Ed Bailey elected by a stealthy ballot-stuffing campaign, Braude let the election process go into hibernation. The Reds Hall of Fame elections were not revived until 1998 when COO John Allen turned the selection process over to the local chapter of the Baseball Writers Association of America. Today, while the Cincinnati BWAA prepare the ballot and serve as a veterans committee, Reds fans are once again allowed to vote in the Hall of Fame elections, either via the Reds website or by paper ballots available at Great American Ball Park.

Another serious problem with the Reds Hall of Fame was that for the longest time it had no proper home. The plaques—made by local metal works company Newman Brothers and as pretty as the ones that hang in the National Baseball Hall of Fame in Cooperstown—were displayed inside Crosley Field, but once the team moved into Riverfront they remained in storage in the bowels of the Stadium. With the construction of the Reds Hall of

Fame building, the plaques could finally be displayed in an appropriate and permanent space.

As for the composition of the membership, some of the previously overlooked but deserving players from the early years—such as Cy Seymour, Bob Ewing, Bid McPhee, Dummy Hoy, Will White, and the Wright brothers—have recently gained admittance. Other deserving old-timers remain on the waiting list—most notably and, as Greg Rhodes has pointed out, most inexplicably, Jake Beckley, who is in the National Baseball Hall of Fame. A clear bias toward players who made significant contributions to championship Reds teams also remains. Of the 66 players in the Reds Hall, 37 of them played on either the 1919 team (6 members), the 1961 team (10), the 1975–1976 teams (10), or the 1940 team (11). Of course, were Pete Rose allowed into the Reds Hall of Fame, as he should be, the 1975–1976 teams would equal the 1940 squad.

There is an element of subjectivity in anything that is voted on, and some players in the Reds Hall of Fame may have been more popular than they were outstanding performers. But who really wants to worry about that? The Reds Hall of Fame is for Reds fans, and according to them the following are the players, managers, and executives who most deserve to be remembered by enshrinement.

| | |
|---|---|
| Paul Derringer—1958 | Ted Kluszewski—1962 |
| Ernie Lombardi—1958 | Rube Bressler—1963 |
| Frank McCormick—1958 | Harry Craft—1963 |
| Johnny Vander Meer—1958 | Heinie Groh—1963 |
| Bucky Walters—1958 | Noodles Hahn—1963 |
| Ival Goodman—1959 | Gus Bell—1964 |
| Eppa Rixey—1959 | Pete Donohue—1964 |
| Ewell Blackwell—1960 | Fred Hutchinson—1965 |
| Edd Roush—1960 | Larry Kopf—1965 |
| Lonny Frey—1961 | Red Lucas—1965 |
| Billy Werber—1961 | Wally Post—1965 |
| Hughie Critz—1962 | Johnny Temple—1965 |
| Bubbles Hargrave—1962 | Jake Daubert—1966 |

Mike McCormick—1966
Billy Myers—1966
Dolf Luque—1967
Bill McKechnie—1967
Sam Crawford—1968
Joe Nuxhall—1968
Warren C. Giles—1969
Jim O'Toole—1970
Roy McMillan—1971
Gordy Coleman—1972
Jim Maloney—1973
Bob Purkey—1974
Smoky Burgess—1975
Brooks Lawrence—1976
Vada Pinson—1977
Frank Robinson—1978
Tommy Helms—1979
Clay Carroll—1980
Leo Cardenas—1981
Wayne Granger—1982
Gary Nolan—1983
Jack Billingham—1984
Johnny Bench—1986

Joe Morgan—1987
Jerry Lynch—1988
Tony Perez—1998
Cy Seymour—1998
Sparky Anderson—2000
Dave Concepcion—2000
Bob Ewing—2001
Mario Soto—2001
Bid McPhee—2002
Don Gullett—2002
George Foster—2003
Dummy Hoy—2003
Ken Griffey Sr.—2004
Bob Howsam—2004
Will White—2004
Eric Davis—2005
Jose Rijo—2005
Harry Wright—2005
George Wright—2005
Tom Browning—2006
Lee May—2006
Tom Seaver—2006

# DUSTY TO THE RESCUE

There's an old adage in baseball that managers get fired on a regular basis because you can't fire the players (at least not all of them at once). The Reds have certainly been living by that rule during their current streak of seven consecutive losing seasons through the end of 2007. Some recent Reds managers—particularly Pete Mackanin, who replaced Jerry Narron halfway through the 2007 campaign—have received better than passing grades from the bleacher and press box critics; yet the Reds brass (CEO Bob Castellini and general manager Wayne Krivsky) decided to take a big swing when it came time to find a new manager to lead Cincinnati into 2008 and beyond, and their decision to hire Dusty Baker in mid-October was regarded by most Reds fans as the home run needed to reverse the club's fortunes.

According to Castellini, the Reds did not hire Baker simply because he was a widely known manager with a proven track record. To be sure, Baker—who formerly served as the field general of the San Francisco Giants and the Chicago Cubs—does come to the job with impressive credentials, including five seasons of 90 or more wins and three Manager of the Year Awards. Nevertheless, Dusty got the job because he impressed Castellini and Krivsky with his knowledge of the game and his desire to win. Baker made it clear during the interview process that he would take the job for one reason and one reason only: to make the Reds into winners again. "I loved to win," he said at the press conference announcing his hiring. "I'm spoiled by winning. I want to get back to that, and I plan on taking this team to the top." Those words were music to the ears of Reds fans, tired of hearing cacophonous excuses for losing lately.

As optimistic and positive-thinking as he is, Baker is also realistic, as his press conference comments indicated. He noted the perennial lack of pitching that has plagued the ballclub for years, and he acknowledged that for the Reds to improve their record they would need to acquire better players. Baker even revealed that, to this end, he was already in contact with players who were interested in coming to Cincinnati to play for the Reds now that he would be filling out the lineup card.

Almost lost in the hoopla  surrounding the Reds' decision was the fact that  Baker was the first African American ever hired to manage the Cincinnati Reds. It was a great honor considering that other eminently qualified former Reds players, such as Frank Robinson, Vada Pinson, Joe Morgan, and Ken Griffey, were never given (for whatever reasons) the opportunity first. Chuck Harmon, the first black player in Reds history, was present at Baker's press conference to proudly mark the historic moment, but Dusty preferred to keep the focus on what he considered to be more important matters. "Hopefully there will come a time when you no longer look at me as an African American manager or

Dusty Baker hopes to end a string of seven straight losing seasons when he takes over as Reds manager in 2008.

leader. You look at me as a man and a leader who's going to lead your team regardless of who I am," he said.

As far as most Reds fans were concerned, Baker's skin color was irrelevant. As the 2007 playoffs and World Series moved along, they were hoping that Baker would have a long and successful career in Cincinnati and one day join Bill McKechnie, Fred Hutchinson, Sparky Anderson, and Lou Piniella as the greatest managers in team history. They were hoping, in other words, that Baker would achieve his immediate goal as described by his agent Greg Genske, who said, "Dusty is extremely excited to join the Cincinnati Reds with its rich history, and looks forward to helping re-establish the legacy of the Big Red Machine."

# TOP 10 BEST TRADES IN REDS HISTORY

There is more than one way to evaluate a baseball trade. One way to judge a trade is by how much the acquired player helped the team win. Another way to judge the trade is by how well the player performed, regardless of whether or not the player helped the team win anything. The following trades made this list because they each helped the Reds win at least a pennant, if not a World Series. The Reds have certainly made other great trades that brought very productive players to the ballclub, but none of them helped achieve the ultimate goal of all good trades—victory—as much as these swaps did.

There are usually interesting stories behind very good or very bad trades, and one example will have to suffice here. Joey Jay had not won more than nine games for the Braves, but he turned out to be the ace of the staff, with a 21–10 record, for the Reds' team that won the 1961 pennant.

Left-handed pitcher Juan Pizarro came along with Jay from the Braves, and the Reds immediately traded him to the Chicago White Sox for Gene Freese, who became the Reds' regular third baseman in 1961. Freese had the best season (.277, 26, 87) of his life in 1961. So the Reds picked up their stopper and a power bat for Roy McMillan, a weak-hitting shortstop they had no trouble replacing. Now that's a great trade! As a footnote to the trade, the Reds might

# HOW THE REDS TRADED JEFF SHAW FOR KEN GRIFFEY JR.

Sometimes a trade can be evaluated right away. After Frank Robinson won the AL Triple Crown in his first year with the Baltimore Orioles, it was obvious the Reds had made a very bad deal. Other times it takes a while for a trade to reveal itself, especially when the trade becomes the first in a series of connected trades that lead to an unforeseen outcome several years down the road.

For instance, signing relief pitcher Jeff Shaw as a free agent on January 2, 1996, was a good move by the Reds, but the club eventually got even more than they bargained for. At the time of his signing, Shaw had a career

**Acquiring Ken Griffey Jr. from the Seattle Mariners in 2000 was a homecoming years in the making.**

record of 11–25 with a 4.50 ERA. The Reds thought he could do better, and he certainly did, pitching well enough to win the Rolaids Relief Man Award for 1997. Shaw became too expensive for the Reds to re-sign, so they dealt him to the Los Angeles Dodgers right before the 1998 All-Star Game for pitcher Dennys Reyes and outfielder–first baseman Paul Konerko.

The Reds really had no place to play the promising young Konerko, so they traded him on November 11, 1998, to the Chicago White Sox for center fielder Mike Cameron.

Then on February 10, 2000, the Reds swapped Cameron, pitcher Brett Tomko, and two minor leaguers to the Seattle Mariners for a player they had coveted for years: Ken Griffey Jr. In this roundabout way, the Reds traded Jeff Shaw for future Hall of Famer Ken Griffey Jr.

By the way, Shaw made the 1998 NL All-Star team as a Cincinnati Red. His trade came after the last game before the three-day All-Star break, so he appeared in Coors Field dressed in the uniform of his new team (the Dodgers) for whom he had never played. It was the first time in baseball history that such a thing had happened.

have done even better in the long run had they kept Pizarro. He won 61 games for the Sox in the first four years after the trade, while Freese suffered a horrible fracture of his ankle during spring training in 1962 and was never the same player again.

1. Joe Morgan, Jack Billingham, Cesar Geronimo, Woody Woodward, and Ed Armbrister from the Houston Astros for Lee May, Tommy Helms, and Jimmy Stewart, Nov. 29, 1971.
2. Edd Roush, Christy Mathewson, and Bill McKechnie from the New York Giants for Buck Herzog and Red Killefer, July 20, 1916.
3. George Foster from the San Francisco Giants for Frank Duffy and Vern Geishert, May 29, 1971.
4. Paul Derringer, Sparky Adams, and Allyn Stout from the St. Louis Cardinals for Leo Durocher, Dutch Henry, and Jack Ogden, May 7, 1933.
5. Bucky Walters from the Philadelphia Phillies for Spud Davis, Al Hollingsworth, and $50,000, June 13, 1938.

6. Heinie Groh, Red Ames, Josh Devore, and $20,000 from the New York Giants for Art Fromme and Eddie Grant, May 22, 1913.
7. Joey Jay and Juan Pizarro from the Milwaukee Braves for Roy McMillan, Dec. 15, 1960.
8. Ernie Lombardi, Babe Herman, and Wally Gilbert from the Brooklyn Dodgers for Tony Cuccinello, Joe Stripp, and Clyde Sukeforth, May 14, 1932.
9. Pedro Borbon, Jim McGlothlin, and Vern Geishert from the California Angels for Alex Johnson and Chico Ruiz, Nov. 25, 1969.
10. Jose Rijo and Tim Birtsas from the Oakland A's for Dave Parker, Dec. 8, 1987.

# THE BAD

The highlights of Reds baseball are so grand, and the good times of Reds baseball have been such darn fun, they tend to overshadow the less successful seasons, teams, and players in club history. But the Reds and their fans have definitely spent time down in the dumps, even if nobody likes to talk about it much.

## THE LOSINGEST REDS TEAM

Whenever some masochist wants to identify the worst team in Reds history, the squad that immediately comes to mind is the Reds brigade that in 1982 became the first in team history to lose 100 or more games. The 101 losses racked up by that hapless group remains the club record. Naturally, the Reds finished in last place, a whopping 28 games behind the division-winning Atlanta Braves (89–73), one of the former punching bags of the Big Red Machine. This plummet to the basement was unexpected to say the least, as the Reds had not pulled up the rear in the National League since 1937; furthermore, the year before the Reds had compiled the best overall record in all of baseball, despite the asinine split-season format, which ultimately denied them a spot in the NL playoffs. In addition, in the previous three years the Reds had compiled the best composite record in the entire National League. Nevertheless, the 1982 season was no illusion: the Reds that year were downright awful.

The mastermind mechanic who finally stripped the gears and seized up the engine of the Big Red Machine was general manager Dick Wagner. It was he who, in refusing to meet the salary demands of the last remnants of the BRM, dispatched to other cities the entire starting outfield of the 1981 team—George Foster, Dave Collins, and Ken Griffey—and replaced them with Cesar Cedeno and three rookies promoted out of the farm system: Paul Householder, Eddie Milner, and Duane Walker. Wagner had also traded Ray Knight to Houston in order to free up third base for Johnny Bench, whose knees and shoulder no longer permitted him to catch on a regular basis. Bench really should have been allowed to transition from catcher to first base, but the latter position was reserved by Wagner for Dan Driessen—the same mediocre talent, ironically, who had somehow inspired the Reds to trade away Tony Perez. All these moves proved to be disastrous. Cedeno showed flashes of brilliance, just as he had for years with the Astros, but as the Reds discovered, he was plagued by inconsistency. Householder and Walker barely hit their weights (.211 and .218) in 1982 and showed during the remainder of their

Johnny Bench's defense at third base was just one of the many problems for the Reds in 1982.

brief major league careers that the Reds had seriously overestimated their potential as major leaguers. Milner's unimpressive .268 on the season turned out to be 15 points above his lifetime average. Bench suffered through what for him was an embarrassment of a season: the worst fielding average among all major league third basemen and paltry offensive stats of .258, 13 homers, and 38 RBIs.

In short, the explosive offense Reds fans had become used to seeing when the Reds batted had been reduced to popguns. The 82 home runs hit by the 1982 Reds was the third lowest total among major league teams, as well as the lowest total turned in by a Reds team since 1946. This power shortage was typified by Driessen, whose 17 home runs led the team, and by the output of the trio of Reds catchers—Alex Trevino, Dave Van Gorder, and Mike O'Berry—who together hit a grand total of one home run. The Reds didn't have any home-run threats on the bench either, as reserves Larry Biittner, Wayne Krenchicki, Mike Vail, Rafael Landestoy, and Tom Lawless combined for nine long balls in 836 at-bats. Worse, the 545 runs scored by the 1982 Reds was the lowest total accumulated by any team in the major leagues that year.

The Reds lineup in 1982 scared no one, other than the Reds pitchers who were forced to labor under the pressure of a constant lack of offensive support. Ace Mario Soto led the team with a 2.79 ERA but struggled to keep his record above .500 at 14–13. Soto, by the way, was not only the sole pitcher on the team to post double-digit wins—he was also the only pitcher besides Ben Hayes at 2–0 to have a winning record at all! Starters Bruce Berenyi and Bob Shirley fashioned decent ERAs (3.36 and 3.60 respectively), but both finished with records well below .500 (9–18 and 8–13 respectively). Even Hall of Famer Tom Seaver couldn't win with this team. Seaver's ERA ballooned to 5.50 and his 5–13 ledger was the first losing record in his long career. The ineptitude of the 1982 Reds didn't permanently scar Seaver though, and he later rebounded with the Chicago White Sox to win 15 games in 1984 and 16 more in 1985.

The 1982 Reds lost 3–2 to the Chicago Cubs on a cold and windy bad omen of an Opening Day. The Cubs were helped by a disputed umpire call that resulted in the ejection of manager John McNamara, and the game was shortened to eight innings because of rain. The Reds lost 10 of their first 13 games and only two weeks into the campaign had fallen 10 games behind the Braves who began the season 13–0. The fate of this bad Reds team was sealed after they lost 20 of 23 games in late June and early July, including nine in a row at one point. Remarkably, the longest winning streak of the year was just four games. The futility of the season was exemplified by a game on June 27. The Reds wasted Mario Soto's brilliant outing of 10 shutout innings against the Braves, and eventually lost the game in 14 innings 2–0 because of their pathetic inability to plate any runs. The Reds hit into seven double plays in the game, tying the major league record. Things were so bad that on July 21, with the Reds firmly ensconced in last place, the *Cincinnati Enquirer* began running a derisive contest that invited fans to predict the day and time that the team would be mathematically eliminated from the pennant race. The newspaper sarcastically announced that the winner of the contest would be awarded two tickets to the final home game of the season, while the runner-up would be awarded four tickets. On July 21, the man who had abruptly fired Sparky Anderson in 1978, Dick Wagner, fired the man he had hired to replace Anderson, John McNamara, and replaced him with coach Russ Nixon. Nixon brought the club home with a slightly better winning percentage (.386) than McNamara had compiled (.370) when he was given the boot, but the difference was all but meaningless, as Reds fans clearly indicated with their absence. Attendance for the year dropped to 1.3 million, an all-time low for Riverfront Stadium, and the one-game nadir came on September 21 when only 6,038 fans bothered to show up for the contest between the Reds and the San Francisco Giants. Most of the players wound up as disillusioned with the disastrous season as Reds fans were, and veteran shortstop Dave Concepcion actually expressed regret at having agreed to play for the team. "If I'd known the Reds were going to let both Foster and Griffey go," he said, "I'd never have signed my new contract."

# THE WORST TEAM IN REDS HISTORY

That 1982 Reds team was bad, but members of the team can take consolation in the fact that they were not the worst Reds team ever. That dubious distinction belongs to the 1934 squad, which was the worst of four consecutive worst teams in Cincinnati major league baseball history. It was during the first half of the 1930s that the Great Depression ravaged America, and Reds baseball in those years was a mirror athletic image of the employment, economic, and financial desolation that plagued households throughout the United States. The Reds finished last four times in a row (1931–1934) with records of 58–96, 60–94, 58–94, and 52–99, for an average of almost 96 losses per year, and this was over a 154-game schedule. Had the 1934 team played the modern schedule of 162 games, they certainly would have beaten the 1982 team to the 100-loss finish line, and it is likely that the 1931–1933 teams would have too. Who could blame Reds fans of the time for being depressed!

In any case, the 1934 team should be considered the most incompetent of this very bad bunch, on the basis of its franchise-worst .344 winning percentage, which translates of course, when we look at the other side of the coin, into a .656 losing percentage!

The 1934 Reds were led, so to speak, by player/manager Bob O'Farrell. In his prime the popular O'Farrell had been one of the best catchers in the National League, and he had even won the NL MVP Award in 1926 as a St. Louis Cardinal for his clutch hitting, his handling of the Cards pitching staff, and his leadership. Unfortunately, by the time O'Farrell took over the Reds, his fourth big-league team (and the second he managed), the flame of desire to win within his breast had burned down to a flicker. Reds general manager Larry MacPhail decided to can O'Farrell in mid-season after he noticed O'Farrell taking the mounting Reds losses with undue equanimity, as evidenced by his hustling out of the clubhouse immediately after the games in order to get in a round of golf before dark. Lou Piniella he was not.

On the other hand, O'Farrell didn't have a lot to work with. The bloated 1934 roster (41 players) was for the most part an uninspiring combination of rookies, journeymen (infielders Tony

Piet and Gordon Slade and outfielder Adam Comorosky), and over-the-hill stars whose best years had been spent with other teams (Cardinals first baseman Jim Bottomley and outfielder Chick Hafey and ex-Dodger pitcher Dazzy Vance). Twenty-three players were tried in the field, and of this group only six had been with the team the year before. Bottomley, Hafey, and catcher Ernie Lombardi were the only returning starters. It was appropriate that the highest batting average on the team of .327 was turned in by rookie outfielder Harlin Pool, who appeared in 99 games after MacPhail purchased him from the Sacramento ballclub in the PCL. Pool, who couldn't field his position, was the quintessential flash in the pan, and after batting .176 in 28 games for the Reds the following year he never made another appearance in the major leagues. There was more continuity on the pitching staff, which featured six holdovers from the year before, including the top three starters, but experience didn't seem to help them. Paul Derringer, who would later become one of the best pitchers in the National League with a good team behind him, was the top winner on the 1934 club with 15 victories, but he lost 21 games (four fewer than he'd lost the previous year with St. Louis and Cincinnati). Benny Frey went 11–16, and Si Johnson joined Derringer in the embarrassing 20-loss club with a slate of 7–22.

The 1934 Reds got off to an even more ominous start than their counterparts of 1982. They lost to the Chicago Cubs at Redland Field 6–0 on Opening Day and were almost no-hit in the process. The Reds lone hit, a single up the middle, came with one out in the ninth inning, and by that time Reds fans were rooting for Cubs pitcher Lon Warneke, who settled for a one-hitter. Obviously, the team gave Reds fans little to cheer about during the rest of the year. At the very end of this dismal season, with Charlie Dressen managing them, the Reds were defeated twice in a three-day period by the St. Louis Cardinals' Dizzy Dean. The decisions were Dean's 29th and 30th victories of the season, and both wins were complete-game shutouts.

Incidentally, that 1934 season came in the midst of a nine-year streak of seasons with a losing record for the Reds. Pretty bad, but

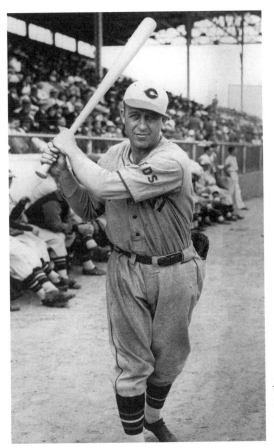

**Jim Bottomley, years past his prime, manned first base for the worst team in Reds history.** (Photo courtesy of Getty Images.)

not the worst in team history. The longest stretch of losing baseball endured by Reds fans came during the period of 1945–1955, when the Reds could not manage to finish .500 or better for 11 straight seasons. Now that's a slump! Bill McKechnie, who had led the Reds to consecutive World Series and a world championship in 1940, was manager when this tailspin started in 1945. John Neun, Bucky Walters, Luke Sewell, and Rogers Hornsby succeeded McKechnie (none successfully), but the Reds never climbed over .500 until 1956, when Birdie Tebbetts guided them to a 91–63 record, good for third place, in his third season at the helm.

Since then the Reds have avoided lengthy strings of losing seasons...until now. The Reds lost considerably more games (90) than they won (72) in 2007, thus saddling them with their seventh consecutive losing season and tying them with the Reds of 1910–1916, who also could not finish a season with more wins than losses during their era of mediocrity. Despite the presence of Ken Griffey Jr., Adam Dunn, Ryan Freel, Brandon Phillips, Aaron Harang, and Bronson Arroyo, the 2007 Reds just did not have enough quality players on the roster to win more games than they lost. A clear indication of this shortage of talent was the fact that the Reds had become token-appearance All-Star Game participants. During the latest string of losing seasons (2001–2007), the Reds have sent only one player to the Midsummer Classic each year, except for 2004, when Griffey, Sean Casey, Barry Larkin, and Danny Graves all made the team. The Reds won-lost record is not likely to improve much until they become better represented at the All-Star Game.

## BAD REDS BATTERS

Of course, there have also been plenty of bad performances turned in by individual Reds players, and the worst Reds players were not necessarily members of the Reds' worst teams. For instance, the only time the Reds had two players on the same team hit under .200 for the season (a minimum of 200 at-bats) was in 1973. The Reds won the National League West Division that year, despite the anemic batting records of shortstop Darrel Chaney, who hit .181 in 227 at-bats, and that of utility infielder Denis Menke, who hit .191 in 241 at-bats. Chaney, by the way, is the only Reds player to hit under .200 in two different seasons—his average in 1969 was .191—and he has the worst career batting average (.207) of any non-pitcher to bat more than 1,000 times in a Reds uniform. In addition to Menke and Chaney, seven other Reds hitters have batted under .200 for a season, and all of them save one were either catchers or shortstops—a clear indication of the historically defensive nature of the two positions. The other weak sticks in Reds history: catcher Bill Bergen (.179 in 1901 and .180 in 1902), shortstop Tommy McMillan (.185 in 1910), shortstop Jimmy Esmond (.195 in 1912), shortstop Frank Emmer (.186 in 1926), shortstop Eddie Miller (.194 in 1946), catcher Johnny Edwards (.191 in 1966), and infielder Nick Esasky (.193 in 1984).

As for power hitting, there are few things less impressive than going through an entire season (minimum 500 at-bats) without hitting a single home run. Since 1920, six Reds have turned the trick, including Heinie Groh (1920), Babe Pinelli (1924), Harry Rice and Jo-Jo Morrissey (1933), and Steve Mesner (1943). Second baseman Johnny Temple did it three times while wearing a Reds uniform—in 1954, 1955, and 1957. Temple did manage to find the seats 15 times during his Reds career (1952–1959), so he is not the worst home-run hitter in club history. That unwanted honor belongs to Morrissey, an infielder who never homered in a Reds uniform. His 803 homerless at-bats (1932–1933) is the Cincinnati Reds career record for at-bats without a homer.

**Adam Dunn has prodigiously racked up home runs and strikeouts during his career with the Reds.**
(Photo courtesy of Getty Images.)

Strikeouts are the ultimate hitting failure, as nothing good but a cool breeze comes from a whiff at the plate, and here too the Reds have had their share of "leaders." Wally Post, Deron Johnson, Lee May, Tony Perez, and George Foster were some of the biggest whiffers in Reds history. Foster struck out 138 times in 1978, May whiffed 142 times in 1969, and Perez racked up more than 100 Ks during eight different seasons while playing in Cincinnati. Bad as they are, those figures can't touch the record of futility being constructed out of thin air by current Reds outfielder Adam Dunn. Reds fans can count on the tall Texan with the big left-handed power stroke for 40 home runs, 100 walks, and 100 RBIs every year; unfortunately, astronomical strikeout totals from Dunn are just as predictable. Dunn set the team record for strikeouts with 170 in his first year with the team (2002). Two years later he set the major league record for Ks with 195. He followed that with totals of 168 and 194 (2006), and he is well on his way—barring a newfound ability to put the bat on the ball or a trade to another team—to passing Tony Perez (with 1,306) and becoming the Reds' career leader in strikeouts.

## BAD REDS PITCHERS

The Reds have also had some stinko pitchers and, unlike many of the Reds worst hitters, the 10 Reds with the lowest winning percentages (based on 100 decisions and a minimum of 900 innings pitched) all played on some of the worst Cincinnati teams. For instance, Tom Hume (.441) and Frank Pastore (.441) toiled for the 1982 Reds; Ray Kolp (.420), Benny Frey (.416), and the all-time Reds loser, Si Johnson (.348), all plied their trade for the 1934 Reds. Curiously, Johnson had his moments of glory, such as the pair of one-hitters he pitched two weeks apart in early 1933, but his career Reds record of 46–86 was even worse than the overall record of the abysmal Reds teams for whom he pitched. The other members of the worst pitchers club: Ken Raffensberger (.473), Jakie May (.466), Herm Wehmeier (.415), Pete Schneider (.410), and Howie Fox (.388). Wehmeier's inclusion in this list is as much a sad story as a matter of record. An all-state football and baseball player at

Cincinnati's Western Hills High School, Wehmeier (1945, 1947–1954) was never able to win consistently for the Reds due largely to his wildness and his penchant for giving up the longball. Reds fans made his life miserable, such that after he was mercifully sold to the Philadelphia Phillies midway through the 1954 season, it was widely repeated that he'd "been booed out of town."

As for bad one-game pitching performances, three of the most horrific came in the same forgettable year: 1901. A 32-year-old right-hander named Bill Phillips, who went 14–18 on the year, should have stayed in the dugout on June 24 because the Phillies hammered him for 22 hits and 19 runs that day. Brooklyn treated Archie Stimmel even worse on September 23: they plated 18 runs against him in only five innings. Worst of all was the effort turned in by Harley "Doc" Parker on June 21, also against the Dodgers. Parker, who'd pitched for the Cubs in the 1890s, was making a comeback to the big leagues and his Reds debut in this game. In eight innings Brooklyn pounded him for 26 hits and 21 runs to set the National League record for one-game hits and runs against a single pitcher. After this debacle, a chastened Parker said, "The next time I get in the box I hope to give a better account of myself." The last-place Reds were bad that year, but not so bad that they even thought twice about letting Parker anywhere near the mound again.

## BAD REDS DEFENSE

Two of the most infamous instances of bad defense in Reds history came at the worst of times. Catcher Ernie Lombardi was the central figure in the first of these episodes, and the setting was Game 4 of the 1939 World Series. With the score tied 4–4 in the top of the tenth inning, the Yankees rallied against Bucky Walters, pitching in relief of starter Paul Derringer. With one out, Frankie Crosetti on third, and Charlie Keller on first, Joe DiMaggio singled to right. Crosetti scored easily, and when Reds right fielder Ival Goodman kicked the ball around, Keller rounded third and kept right on going. Keller and Goodman's throw arrived simultaneously. The collision between Keller and

## DID YOU KNOW...

That Ernie Lombardi (1932–1941), called "Schnozz" for his big nose, was so slow that infielders could play him very deep and throw him out at first on ground balls that would have been hits for most other batters? Still, the catcher hit .311 during his time with the Reds, and he won the 1938 National League MVP Award.

Lombardi, trying to block the plate, knocked the ball out of Lombardi's glove, and Keller was safe. As Lombardi lay sprawled in the dirt with the baseball resting a few feet away, DiMaggio sped around the bases and scored behind Keller all the way from first base. Three runs scored on the play, the Yankees won the game 7–4, and Lombardi was reviled for his part in the play, which became known as "Lombardi's Snooze," as if the catcher had simply been too mentally slow to react to DiMaggio's dash home. The play seriously damaged Lombardi's reputation, and as time went by, fans ignorant of the situation and the Yankees' four-game sweep assumed that the play had cost the Reds the World Series. In fact, Lombardi had been kicked in the groin during the collision with Keller and thus rendered momentarily incapacitated. The runs scored by both Keller and DiMaggio were actually Goodman's fault, and neither cost the Reds the game anyway, and certainly not the Series. Nevertheless, the image of a woozy Reds catcher lying helplessly in the dirt as Yankees base runners flew around the bases is the one which still carries the day. Lombardi, who was already the subject of ridicule for his huge nose and his slowness afoot, was just too easy a target. Goodman, as well as Walters and any of the Reds infielders who might have covered the plate while Lombardi was down, have escaped censure for their culpability.

The eyes of the baseball world are always focused on Cincinnati on Opening Day, and Reds infielder Pokey Reese chose the 1998 Opening Day game to showcase his fallibility with the leather. Reese, a natural second baseman, was starting at shortstop for Barry Larkin, who was sitting out the game against the Padres because of injury. Reese made it perfectly clear that Larkin's job was not in jeopardy by committing four errors, tying a major league record. Reese's first error came in the first inning when his throw to first on a double-play ball sailed into the dugout. His second came in the third when he fumbled a routine grounder. Errors number three and four came after that on the same play. With runners on second and third, Reese bobbled a grounder off the bat of Tony Gwynn, which allowed Gwynn to reach first. Reese then literally kicked the baseball while trying to corral it, which allowed the runner on second to take third, giving him three errors in the inning and four for the game. The errors helped San Diego take a 3–0 lead over the Reds, and Cincinnati wound up losing the game 10–2. Afterward, Reese poked fun at himself by observing that he'd had a worse day than the poor fellow with

Pokey Reese got off to a historic start in 1988, recording four errors on Opening Day.

the giant pooper scooper who'd trailed the elephant in the Opening Day parade. Reese, of course, recovered from this one-game disaster to become a Gold Glove second baseman for the Reds in 1999 and 2000.

## BAD WHEN IT COUNTS THE MOST

A player's performance is magnified when the games mean the most, and bad performances that would go overlooked during the long regular season become burned into the memory during the postseason like a wanted poster on a telephone pole. When bad hitting during the postseason is the subject, the Reds player who comes immediately to mind is outfielder Reggie Sanders. During the 1995 Division Series against the Los Angeles Dodgers and then the NLCS against the Atlanta Braves, Sanders went a combined 4-for-29 for a .138 average. Pretty bad, but what made it even worse and a scandalously inept performance from the fans' point of view was that Sanders struck out 19 times! Opposing pitchers discovered that Sanders had trouble with the high fastball, and they exploited the weakness to the hilt. Some experts predicted that such a dismal performance would destroy the confidence of a young player such as Sanders, but Reggie rebounded to put together a solid career, although not all of it came as a Cincinnati Red.

Furthermore, a peek at Reds history shows that Sanders was not the first Cincinnati batter to roll over at the worst possible time. The Reds lost the 1939 World Series to the Yankees because they couldn't score any runs. Three of the culprits in that batting debacle were left fielder Wally Berger (0-for-15), second baseman Lonny Frey (0-for-17), and center fielder Harry Craft (1-for-11). Add 'em up, and you get a 1-for-43 showing, bad enough to doom almost any team in a short series. And don't forget Tony Perez, who went 1-for-18 (.056 average) in the 1970 World Series; Ken Griffey who went 1-for-17 (.059) in the 1976 Series; or Hal Morris, who went 1-for-14 (.071) in the 1990 Series. Those were three of the best players to ever wear a Reds uniform, which just goes to show that in baseball anybody can have a bad day...or a bad week, season, or career!

# RECORD REDS BAD

In baseball there is bad, and then there's record-setting bad. No player or team wants any of the latter, but if you play long enough, some record-setting bad is almost inevitable, and the Reds have had their share of it. On offense, the strikeout is about as bad as it gets. Even a ground-out may produce a run, although the batter is not credited with an RBI when he hits into a double play. And by the way, the Reds seasonal record for twin-killings is held by catcher Ernie Lombardi who grounded into 30 DPs in 1938. Ernie was kind of slow afoot, but you probably figured that one out.

As for strikeouts, Tony Perez is the Reds' all-time strikeout king, with 1,306. But don't worry, Tony. Adam Dunn is right behind you and is scheduled to pass you as if you are standing still in early 2009. If he's not traded first, the Dunnster will leave his name all over the Reds record book in strikeout categories. He already has a good—or bad—start. The Reds record for Ks in one game (5) is shared by Eric Davis and Dunn, although Davis whiffed five times in an extra-inning game, while Adam K-ed five times in a regular nine inning affair (on August 20, 2002, at Arizona). Adam holds the Reds' single-season record for Ks by a left-handed batter with 195 (2004), although Mike Cameron gets credit for the record for right-handers (145 in 1999). Dunn was also a member of the 2004 team that set the club record for strike-outs in one season (1,335), and he was the leader of the pack (with 168 Ks) that set the Reds record for most players (5) with 100 or more Ks in the same season a year later. The other members of that group were Wily Mo Pena (116), Felipe Lopez (111), Austin Kearns (107), and Jason LaRue (101). Finally, the Reds team record for strikeouts in a game is 18 (accomplished twice), which thankfully Adam Dunn had nothing to do with. On August 26, 1998, the Reds went down swinging 18 times against the Chicago Cubs at Riverfront Stadium. Kerry Wood, the hottest young pitcher in baseball at the time who had earlier in the season struck out 20 in a game, racked up 16 of those Ks. The Reds also struck out 18 times in a game on July 14, 1968, and the Astros' Don Wilson notched every one of them. Wilson's dominating performance was no fluke, as he no-hit the Reds a year later.

There have also been some peculiarly bad Reds pitching performances worth noting. During a 7–0 loss to the Dodgers in Los Angeles in a 1963 game, Jim Owens set the team record for balks in one inning with three. Jim argued a little too heatedly after the third balk, and the umpires sent him to the showers early. Bud Podbielan set the team record for walks in a game by one pitcher with 13 on May 18, 1953. Bud also gave up six hits and hit a batter, but with Brooklyn Dodgers all over the bases all day long he still pulled out a win, 2–1, on a Ted Kluszewski home run in the bottom of the tenth inning. The team record for runs allowed in one game is 25, set on September 23, 1901, when the Reds lost to the Dodgers 25–6 at League Park in Cincinnati. Archie Stimmel gave up 18 of those runs in five innings. Even worse from an emotional point of view was the game on August 8, 1954, when the Reds lost 20–7 to the Dodgers in Brooklyn. Dem Bums scored 13 runs that day in the eighth inning, 12 of them after there were two outs. Ouch! Even more remarkable, the major league record for home runs allowed in one inning is five. It has been done four times in National League history, and the Reds were the benefactors each time. Most recently the Reds did it on April 22, 2006, at Milwaukee when Brandon Claussen surrendered four homers and Chris Hammond one to Brewers batters in the fourth inning of an 11–0 loss. Even worse statistically was the five-homer-in-one-inning game of August 23, 1961, when the San Francisco Giants beat the Reds 14–0 at Crosley Field. In that debacle the Giants scored 12 runs in the ninth inning, and in the process set the modern major league record for total bases in one inning with 27. In that painfully memorable ninth inning, Joe Jay gave up home runs to Orlando Cepeda and Felipe Alou; Jim Brosnan gave up a homer to Jim Davenport; and Bill Henry gave up homers to Willie Mays and Johnny Orsino.

Finally, 1956 should be remembered as a good year for exorcising some bad attendance in Reds history. For that year the Reds became the final major league team to surpass the 1 million mark in season attendance with 1,125,928. The Reds' highest season attendance before 1956 was the 981,443 drawn in 1939. Starting in 1970, the Reds have never drawn fewer than 1 million fans in a season, and the club's all-time high of 2,629,708 came more than 20 years ago, in 1976.

# TOP 10 WORST TRADES IN REDS HISTORY

As shrewd a hand as the Reds have played in making player deals, it would not be realistic to expect the club not to have made at least a few bad trades over the long course of the team's history. The trades by which Christy Mathewson and Frank Robinson left the Reds are two of the worst deals in baseball history. Every Reds fan knows about the disastrous Robinson deal; few even know that the Reds owned Mathewson for a short time. The Reds acquired Mathewson for $100 in a minor league draft after the New York Giants had returned the green pitcher (0–3 in six games for the 1900 Giants) to the Norfolk, Virginia, club. When ballclubs in the newly formed American League began trying to pry Mathewson away from the Reds, the Giants changed their minds and decided they wanted Mathewson back. They dangled star pitcher Amos Rusie (245–174 lifetime) in front of the Reds, who took the bait even though Rusie was recovering from a sore arm. Rusie turned out to be finished, pitching in only three games for the Reds before calling it quits; Mathewson went on to become one of the greatest pitchers in history, compiling a 373–188 record with an ERA of 2.13. The Reds might have recognized Mathewson's great talent and held onto him, but they never even tried him out for some reason.

Following are some other personnel blunders, including trading first baseman Joe Adcock, who hit 305 home runs after leaving the Reds; reliever John Wetteland, later a top closer with 330 career saves; and Claude Osteen, who went on to win 196 games in the majors, twice turning in 20-win seasons for the Los Angeles Dodgers.

1. Christy Mathewson to the New York Giants for Amos Rusie, Dec. 15, 1900.
2. Frank Robinson to the Baltimore Orioles for Milt Pappas, Jack Baldschun, and Dick Simpson, Dec. 9, 1965.

3. Joe Adcock to the Milwaukee Braves for Rocky Bridges and cash, Feb. 16, 1953.
4. John Wetteland and Bill Risley to the Montreal Expos for Dave Martinez, Scott Ruskin, and Willie Greene, Dec. 11, 1991.
5. Claude Osteen to the Washington Senators for Dave Sisler and cash, Sept. 16, 1961.
6. Hank Sauer and Frankie Baumholtz to the Chicago Cubs for Harry Walker and Peanuts Lowrey, June 15, 1949.
7. Curt Flood and Joe Taylor to the St. Louis Cardinals for Marty Kutyna, Ted Wieand, and Willard Schmidt, Dec. 5, 1957.
8. Dutch Ruether to the Brooklyn Dodgers for Rube Marquard, Dec. 15, 1920.
9. Don Hoak, Smoky Burgess, and Harvey Haddix to the Pittsburgh Pirates for Whammy Douglas, Jim Pendleton, Frank Thomas, and Johnny Powers, Jan. 30, 1959.
10. Hal McRae and Wayne Simpson to the Kansas City Royals for Roger Nelson and Richie Scheinblum, Nov. 30, 1972.

## THE MAYOR'S WILD WILD PITCH

Over the years Reds fans have witnessed a lot of ceremonial first pitches, thrown by famous Hall of Famers (Jackie Robinson), U.S. presidents (George W. Bush), and all sorts of other dignitaries and VIPs. Without a doubt the most memorable first pitch of them all has to be the one let fly on Opening Day 2007 at Great American Ball Park by Cincinnati mayor Mark Mallory. Memorable in a bad, pathetic, "worse than a second-grader throwing off the wrong foot" kind of way.

Reds fans would have been forewarned had they known that Mayor Mallory had practiced throwing for weeks prior to the game. Any former athlete would only need to warm up, not practice for weeks, in order to make a decent toss of about 50 feet. Unfortunately, the mayor was no former athlete, and he found the thought of having to perform in front of a sellout crowd a bit unnerving, to say the least. To make matters worse, everybody from Pete Rose to the Reds mascots teased him about the pressure of the situation before the game.

In 2007, Cincinnati mayor Mark Mallory uncorked the most infamous first pitch in Reds history. (Photo courtesy of Getty Images.)

Mallory warmed up in privacy beneath the grandstands, and when it was time to do the honors, he strode out to the middle of the diamond and climbed atop the pitching mound, as if he were going to throw the first pitch from the rubber. Thankfully, he stepped down and moved up to right in front of the mound where first-pitchers traditionally make their ceremonial toss. The decreased distance didn't help: Mallory's pitch to former Reds great Eric Davis standing at home plate didn't come close. It bounced about halfway between the politician and the ballplayer and also went wide-left about 10 feet. The throw was so bad that the crowd booed, Davis laughed, and umpire Randy Marsh jokingly threw Mallory out of the game.

As terrible as the throw was, it became a godsend for the pundits. The headline on the front page of the *Cincinnati Enquirer* the next day said: "Imagine if Mallory hadn't practiced First Pitch." Reds broadcaster and former pitcher Chris Welsh added, "I will say that he already has a gift for a terrific pick-off move. I wish I had a pitch that moved that much." And former Reds publicity director Jon Braude, who himself once tossed a not-so-good first pitch, added, "Mine was bad, but it was nowhere near as bad as the one yesterday. It was almost a new example of the hidden-ball trick."

Fortunately, Mayor Mallory was a good sport about the embarrassing performance. His office released a list of the top 10 reasons for his blooper pitch, and he willingly accepted a couple of invitations to appear on national TV. He did one interview with ESPN2's *Cold Pizza* and booked a do-over on *Jimmy Kimmel Live*. When asked if Kimmel would be his catcher for the talk-show toss, Mallory replied, "If so, he'd better watch his nose." The mayor also shrewdly planned to do what he could to help Cincinnati while he had the nation's attention. "Who would've thought such a bad pitch could bring such good attention to the city of Cincinnati?" he said. "I have an opportunity to talk about great things that are going on in the city." For that type of thinking, Cincinnatians finally applauded their mayor.

## Mayor Mallory's Top 10 Excuses

10. I have a shoulder injury from cracking the whip on city council.
9. I got some last-minute advice from Lou Piniella [Cubs manager on Opening Day 2007 and former Reds manager].
8. I was protesting Ken Griffey's move to right field [which Griffey himself objected to].
7. I didn't want to show up President Bush. He might put a wiretap on me.
6. I am saving my best stuff for my Bengals tryout.
5. First pitch? I thought I was throwing out the first bowling ball.
4. I grew up in the West End playing on concrete. A field with grass and dirt threw me off.
3. Eric Davis's red shoes blinded me.
2. My best sport is Putt-Putt.
1. Eric Davis missed the sign. I called for a pitchout.

# THE UGLY

As indicated previously, into the life of every ballclub a little bad must fall, as in "Honey, I had a bad day at the office." Which is surely what a player says after he strikes out five times in a single game, as did Adam Dunn on August 20, 2002, against the Arizona Diamondbacks to tie the Reds record, originally set by Eric Davis on April 25, 1987, against the Houston Astros. Bad in baseball just happens. It is inevitable, as no team or player can always be at their best. And fans are for the most part pretty understanding, and usually ready to give their team and its players another chance. Ugly is a different matter altogether, as it has less to do with skill and talent and the vicissitudes of competition at the very highest level and more to do with character...or the lack thereof. Yes, ugly has to do with behavior—with the way people adhere or don't adhere to the highest ethical and moral standards; with the way they treat other people; and with the way they handle disagreements, disappointment, and defeat (or the prospect of defeat). The Cincinnati Reds are an honorable franchise with a great deal to be proud of, but as we shall see, they have suffered letdowns, embarrassments, and sins. Like every other major league ballclub, the Reds have had their fair share of ugly.

# THE 1919 CINCINNATI BLACKLEGS?

The Reds were intimately involved in the ugliest event in baseball history, bar none: the 1919 Black Sox scandal, so-called because the Chicago White Sox laid down in the Fall Classic that year for money. Nothing the Reds and its personnel and followers have done before or since can compare to this catastrophic calamity. The sordid affair threatened to ruin baseball and obliterate its standing as America's national pastime. For many years the Reds were perceived to be merely innocent bystanders to the treachery that the White Sox players and the gamblers were involved in; the Reds were victims just as much as the honest baseball fan. Any ensuing stain upon the franchise's honor was thought to be accidental. In recent years, as historians have more closely examined the evidence surrounding the events of the day and the testimony of participants in those events, it has become increasingly clear that the Reds were possibly not as innocent as previously believed.

Of course, the one thing that is beyond dispute is the dishonesty of the White Sox. The fixing of ballgames by gamblers had long been a thorn in the side of Major League Baseball, and rumors that one team or another in the World Series was not playing honestly were almost an annual occurrence in the fall. In 1919 the rumors were true. The White Sox were a veteran powerhouse of a team that had conquered the dominant of the two major leagues, the American. All was not well in Chicago, however. The White Sox were owned by the arrogant skinflint Charles Comiskey, who paid his players more like cellar dwellers than champions, and the simmering anger of his players over such treatment became the embers of resentment that the gamblers were able to coax into a blaze of greed and revenge.

The idea of fixing the 1919 World Series by capitalizing on the turmoil and bitterness that plagued the White Sox originally came from a group of small-time gamblers from St. Louis and Des Moines, Iowa. They enlisted the help of some more prominent gamblers from the East, including a couple of former major leaguers who had access to the Sox players, and eventually the most prominent gambler in the country, Arnold Rothstein, nicknamed "The Big Bankroll," got behind the scheme. By the time the Series neared, rumors that the fix was in had become a roar that only the deaf could not hear. The smart money on the street knew that the White Sox were going to lie down, and the Reds, who had previously been considered no match for the Sox, were now the heavy favorites to win the Series.

At least six White Sox players joined the conspiracy: star pitchers Eddie Cicotte and Lefty Williams, first baseman Chick Gandil, shortstop Swede Risberg, center fielder Happy Felsch, and utility infielder Fred McMullin. To this day, controversy surrounds the question of whether or not a seventh player, the legendary Shoeless Joe Jackson, actively participated in the fix. Since Jackson was the best hitter on the team—indeed he was one of the two or three best hitters in all of baseball—the gamblers keenly wanted his big bat taken out of the equation. Jackson did accept a payment, but he had a change of heart before the games began and tried to return the money to Comiskey, who refused to take the wad of cash, to accept Jackson's apology, or even to admit to his knowledge of the ugly shenanigans under way. Based on his performance during the Series—Jackson led all hitters with a .375 average—some historians believe Jackson did his best; others believe that Jackson was simply good at camouflaging his intentional failures. In either case, a year later, after baseball's new commissioner, Judge Kenesaw Mountain Landis, cleaned up the mess like an avenging angel, Jackson was banned from baseball for life, along with the six completely willing participants and an eighth player, third baseman Buck Weaver, who did not participate in the fix but knew of it and did not report it.

The White Sox players should have known better than to trust gamblers—what happened once the Series began only made the whole sorry episode more pathetic, more ironic, and much, much uglier. In essence, the gamblers double-crossed the players. The crooks gave the crooked players only token payments of the agreed-to $100,000 bribe total and assurances of future payments. Already too involved to back out, the White Sox went ahead with the fix and promptly lost the first two games in Cincinnati in suspicious fashion. (The sign that the fix was on was for the first Reds batter in Game 1 to be hit with a pitch. When control expert

Cicotte plunked Reds leadoff batter Morrie Rath in the back, the money bet on the Reds to win the Series flowed in.) Angry at being impudently suckered, the Black Sox decided to double-cross their double-crossers, played honestly in Game 3 at home and won, but after receiving some more token payments they sold some more of their souls to the devil and dropped the fourth and fifth games, also played in Chicago.

Because World War I had curtailed the previous season, the powers-that-be had agreed to a nine-game World Series for 1919 in order to recoup some of the gate proceeds lost during 1918. At this point, with the teams returning to Cincinnati, the Reds needed only one more victory to capture the Series. It was at this juncture that the fans' expectations were really turned upside down and that suspicions of dishonesty attached like leeches to some of the Reds players.

Championship fever ran high in the Queen City, noisy and enthusiastic Reds fans jammed Redland Field, the Reds brimmed with confidence, and they had well-rested pitchers to throw. They lost Games 6 and 7 to throw the whole affair into total confusion, giving Chicago fans hope that their team had righted itself and would now take the final two contests to complete a come-from-behind Series victory. Were the Sox trying to win now, or was something else going on? Well, Dutch Ruether, the Reds starter in Game 6, had been seen openly conversing with known gamblers before and during the World Series. And then, before Game 7, Reds starter and loser that day, Slim Sallee, admitted to manager Pat Moran and center fielder Edd Roush that he had been directly propositioned by gamblers the night before. Even though Sallee claimed to have angrily rebuffed the proposition, a pall fell over the Cincinnati ballclub at the thought that some of the Reds might have become as crooked as the Black Sox. Perhaps, the thinking went, some Reds players felt that the team's big lead gave them the opportunity to make some extra (albeit tainted) money without causing the team to ultimately lose the Series. Adding to the retrospective suspicions, attendance for Game 7 was extremely low, and some have interpreted this as an indication that Reds fans knew their team was going to intentionally lose, thereby lengthening the Series and

# DID YOU KNOW...

That Edd Roush (1916–1926, 1931) was a habitual latecomer to Reds spring training, partly because he always felt he deserved a higher salary than the Reds were offering, but partly because he simply hated spring training workouts?

increasing each player's share of the gate receipts. On the other hand, Reds fans may have stayed away from Game 7 because they were disappointed with the loss in Game 6, or because—and this is a much more likely explanation—the team did not have a very efficient network of outlets and processes to sell tickets for Game 7, starting the morning of the game, after having sold tickets for Games 1, 2, and 6 as packages before the start of the Series.

When the teams returned to Chicago, the Series reverted to form. Disgusted, disheartened, and perhaps beginning to absorb some notion of the eternal shame they were bringing down upon themselves, some (at least) of the crooked White Sox players wanted to go ahead and complete the double-cross of the double-crossing gamblers and win the Series. But it was too late for that. As star Sox pitcher Lefty Williams later testified in court, thugs threatened his life and that of his wife the night before the game if Williams didn't follow through on the fix. The next day, Williams, who had won 23 games in the regular season while turning in an ERA of 2.64, didn't make it out of the first inning. The Reds scored four times in the first and won the game 10–5. A year later, after rumors of the fix failed to die down, the Black Sox and some of the gamblers were put on trial for conspiracy. Hamstrung by lost documents, retracted confessions, and the disappearances of many of the principal gamblers, the trial was a farce, and the players were found not guilty; however, it was only a temporary reprieve, obliterated by Landis's famous pronouncement:

> Regardless of the verdicts of juries, no player who throws a ballgame, no player that undertakes or promises to

throw a ballgame, no player that sits in conference with a bunch of crooked players and gamblers where the ways and means of throwing games are discussed and does not promptly tell his club about it, will ever play professional baseball.

Reds fans were ecstatic at the team's first world championship, but many of the Reds players, especially Edd Roush, resented the implication that seemed to attach itself to the victory: that the Reds won only because the White Sox intentionally lost. Despite his suspicions about the honesty of some of his teammates, Roush always insisted that the Reds had the better team and would have beaten the White Sox under any circumstances. The complete and exact truth about the 1919 World Series—which games were thrown, on which plays did players not try their hardest, what

In recent years, baseball historians have begun taking a closer look at the Reds' involvement in the Black Sox scandal of 1919. (Photo courtesy of Getty Images.)

was the total impact of the dishonest playing on the outcome—these things will never be known. The irony of ironies involving the Reds' honesty (or lack thereof) comes down to an unpalatable choice: contrary to Roush's opinion, if the Reds played the entire Series on the level, it's likely the White Sox would have won it. On the other hand, if gamblers did compromise some key Reds players whose failures were intentional, the Reds may safely be considered to have been equally as talented as the Black Sox, but equally as dishonest, too. Either way, the 1919 world championship won by the Reds is one which will forever be tainted.

## THE ROSE SCANDAL AND AFTERWARD

Commissioner Landis came down hard on the Black Sox because he knew that baseball would be destroyed as the national pastime if the public were to ever lose confidence in the honesty of the competition. After the Black Sox scandal, permanent notices warning about the consequences of gambling went up in the clubhouse of every professional baseball team, and no one dared to ignore the warnings for the next five decades. Yet in the last half of the 1980s, baseball's well was again poisoned by gambling, and the person responsible for the sabotage was, incredibly, a Cincinnati Red: the once famous, now infamous, Pete Rose.

Despite his fall from grace, Pete Rose remains the most popular player in Cincinnati Reds history, and the reasons for his popularity are not hard to figure out. Rose is a native son who came up the hard way, fighting for everything he has been able to squeeze out of life. In uniform, Rose was the consummate self-made ballplayer who redefined the idea of hustle and sought victory as the only worthwhile goal, an attitude exemplified by his steamrolling of catcher Ray Fosse to win the 1970 All-Star Game at Riverfront Stadium. (Think we will ever see a player risk life, limb, and fortune to do something like that again? Not a chance, judging by Alex Rodriguez's polite "Go ahead and tag me out" surrender to the Dodgers' Russell Martin at home plate during the 2007 All-Star Game in San Francisco.) Unpretentious, overachieving, and unstoppable, Cincinnati's Rose became the face of the franchise and of the city itself. His popularity crested when he became the all-time hits leader on September 11, 1985, and a contented future as Reds manager and a surefire first-ballot Hall of Fame selection seemed to stretch beckoningly before him. How wrong that picture was!

Reds fans never realized it, but the seeds of Rose's demise were planted during the same hardscrabble youth that produced his indomitable will to win and succeed. Petty though it was, gambling had always been a part of Rose's environment. Rose idolized his father, a tough semipro football player and humble bank teller, and Harry Rose was a habitual gambler on dog and horse races. According to one theory, Rose turned to gambling to replace the thrill of competition, which he no longer had once he retired as a player, but evidence eventually surfaced to support the case that Rose bet on baseball even while he was still an active player. Whenever his addiction started, once Rose began gambling on baseball, a rogue's gallery of criminals became his inner circle of friends. And in fact, it was the legal troubles of those friends that dragged Rose's secret life into the light of day. The FBI was after several of Rose's friends for tax evasion and drug dealing, and after Pete's name came up repeatedly during their investigations, the FBI passed on what they had learned about Rose's gambling to the baseball hierarchy.

Commissioner Peter Ueberroth summoned Rose to a meeting in New York on February 20, 1989, in order to question him about the rumors of his gambling. Here, at the very beginning of the unraveling of Rose's career and life, is where the die was cast. If Rose had come clean, repented, and placed himself at the mercy of the commissioner, he might have saved himself, despite the seeming inevitability that baseball's death penalty would have been immediately lowered upon him like the blade of a guillotine. If Pete had been paying attention, he would have noticed that the complete rehabilitation of criminals and transgressors of all sorts had become a national recreation in America, especially when the offenders repented (usually tearfully) and were canny enough to lay the blame for their sins on some kind of disease or condition they had been helpless to resist. Surely, Rose could have been

# THE REDS' UGLIEST GAME

If one Reds game can be singled out as the ugliest, a leading candidate would have to be the last game of the 1902 season, which the Reds played against the Pirates in Pittsburgh on October 4. The Reds did not want to play the game because it was a cold day and the field was a quagmire due to a long morning rain. Although the Pirates had already clinched the National League pennant, they insisted on playing the game because they wanted to notch their 103rd win of the season, which would set a new league record. Forced to go ahead with the meaningless game, Reds player/manager Joe Kelley played most of his players out of position, which turned the contest into a travesty. Two outfielders and a first baseman (Mike Donlin, Cy Seymour, and Jake Beckley) took turns on the mound for Cincinnati, while Kelley played three left-handers in the infield and positioned pitcher Rube Vickers behind the plate. Even worse than the musical chairs positioning, the Reds hardly put forth their best efforts. Kelley and Seymour smoked cigarettes on the field during the game, and Vickers allowed a record six passed balls in his two innings behind the dish. Vickers's antics in particular infuriated the crowd. He barely reached for any pitches that were not right over the plate, and he took his time ambling after the six passed balls to howls of laughter from his teammates. While retrieving one passed ball, he even took out a handkerchief and loudly blew his nose. The Pirates had no trouble winning the game, 11–2, but afterward owner Barney Dreyfuss refunded all ticket money in order to keep the Pittsburgh fans from rioting in disgust. Reds owner Garry Herrmann was so embarrassed by the pathetic show put on by his players that he returned the Cincinnati portion of the gate receipts.

forgiven after having been properly chastised, at least to the point that his eligibility for being considered for the National Baseball Hall of Fame would have been preserved. But as we all know, it was simply not in Rose's nature to admit fault, to show weakness, or to accept defeat.

Pete Rose chose to fight. He took lawyers with him to New York, and denied almost everything, admitting only that he bet on an occasional football or basketball game. Rose relied on denial and legal wrangling throughout the long and agonizing summer ahead, but they were not a sufficient defense, and in the end, on August 23, backed into a corner by the Dowd Report and the righteous determination of new commissioner Bart Giamatti to protect baseball at all costs, Rose accepted the deal that has haunted him to this day: lifetime banishment from the game with permission to apply for reinstatement after one year. The agreement also stipulated no finding that Rose was guilty of having bet on baseball, but that Pyrrhic victory for Rose was undercut the very next day when Giamatti told reporters that, yes, he did believe, based on the evidence, that Rose had bet on baseball.

The events following the climax of the Rose betting scandal seemed to have been scripted for the most outlandish of soap operas. Nine days after Rose accepted the deal, Giamatti suffered a massive heart attack and died. The stress of dealing with the Rose scandal almost certainly contributed to Giamatti's passing, and most observers believe that current baseball commissioner Bud Selig, a good friend of Giamatti's, holds Giamatti's death against Rose. As for Rose, he had already resigned as manager of his hometown Reds, but things then got even worse. In early 1990, the IRS conducted an exhaustive investigation into Rose's income, and on April 16 Charlie Hustle pleaded guilty to two counts of filing false income tax returns. Later that summer Rose was fined $50,000 and sentenced to five months in prison. Becoming a common jailbird was a bitter embarrassment, but nothing Rose could not handle. What would turn out to be much worse for his psyche and reputation in the long run was the National Baseball Hall of Fame's board of directors' decision, little noticed at the time, to make anyone on baseball's ineligible list—such as Pete Rose—also ineligible for induction into the Hall.

Rose served his time quietly, and as the years passed taking his punishment like a man won him considerable sympathy. In fact, there were calls for him to be forgiven and reinstated, issued by those who felt that his ordeal had gone on long enough. And Rose remained, somehow, extremely popular with

Pete Rose's many accomplishments on the field have been overshadowed by his bad judgment off the field.

a large segment of the baseball fan population. He was voted onto the honorary All-Century Team in a promotion sponsored by MasterCard, and at a ceremony honoring the members of the team he received the largest ovation of any player. Later, a normally boring celebrity softball game at soon-to-be-demolished Riverfront Stadium turned into an electric sellout as Reds fans turned out en masse to say good-bye and watch the old hustler play ball one last time. (Rose did not disappoint, and his head-first slide into third brought back many happy memories.) Rose was his own worst enemy, though. Despite pleas from his best friends in baseball (e.g., Joe Morgan and Mike Schmidt) for him to come clean and admit the truth, Rose refused to change his story. He also showed an appalling lack of good judgment in failing to realize how arrogant and unrepentant he looked when he did things such as openly gamble at racetracks and in Las

Vegas, joke about his gambling on television talk shows, and appear in Cooperstown on Induction Weekend to sell autographs and hawk merchandise while supporters could sign petitions calling for his reinstatement. Rose managed to obtain a few meetings with Selig, but none of them ever produced the desired result. He changed course in early 2004 when he finally admitted that he had bet on baseball in a cheesy confessional called *My Prison without Bars*, as told to Rick Hill. The timing of the book's release angered some people in baseball as it coincided with, and thus upstaged, the announcement of the Hall of Fame elections of Paul Molitor and Dennis Eckersley. The book itself hardly helped Rose, as most readers found it to be spectacularly self-serving and insincere. Even while admitting his guilt, Rose attacked the findings of the Dowd Report—comparing himself and his sins to other, supposedly worse transgressors and their transgressions—and tried to deflect responsibility for his actions by claiming he was a victim of a gambling addiction and Attention-Deficit Hyperactivity Disorder.

Rose has continued to periodically make himself a news story to the present day, but unfortunately his remarks and actions invariably continue to highlight the worst, not the best, sides of his personality and character. In September of 2006, for example, the *New York Daily News* reported that some very unusual Rose autographed baseballs were going to be sold by a major sports memorabilia auction house. The baseballs bore the inscription "I'm sorry I bet on baseball—Pete Rose," and the auction company had 30 of the balls for sale. That total turned out to be only a small portion of the balls available. Several sources confirmed that Rose had signed 303 of the apology balls, the number corresponding cutely to his lifetime batting average. It was also learned that some of the balls were already on the market, a few of them supposedly having been sold for as much as $10,000 each. Once the story got out, Rose tried to exercise some damage control, offering an explanation that portrayed his actions as something other than another tawdry attempt to make money off of the betrayal referred to in the inscription. Rose claimed that he had inscribed and signed the baseballs for two friends, at their request, and that the friends were supposed to have put the balls away for 15 or 20 years—the implication being that Rose was not intended to be the one to reap a financial windfall from the sale of the balls with the sensational inscription. But then we learned that Rose was selling some of the special apology baseballs himself on his own website, PeteRose.com, at $299 a pop.

Another embarrassing moment for Rose occurred on July 9, 2007, when, as part of a series celebrating *USA Today*'s 25th anniversary, the paper published its list of the 25 top sports scandals to occur in the past 25 years. The nation's newspaper named the Rose betting scandal the worst, ahead of other sorry episodes, such as a college basketball point-shaving scheme, two different Olympic bribery cases, the Duke lacrosse fiasco, the brawl between the Indiana Pacers and Detroit Pistons fans, the ongoing BALCO/ steroids crisis, and even the O.J. Simpson murder case!

The latest, but surely not the last, public relations disaster for Rose came at the end of July 2007, when Rose appeared at a summer baseball camp run jointly by the Reds and the U.S. Army. While Jim O'Toole and Bronson Arroyo each spoke about 20 minutes and gave the kids some good advice, such as the value of playing catch in the backyard with their dads, Rose bored the kids and their parents, too, by rambling on for almost an hour. Worse, he told some age-inappropriate jokes that were in poor taste and, according to reports in the *Cincinnati Enquirer,* repeatedly used obscene and vulgar language, as if he were trying to entertain a half-drunk nightclub crowd, not a group of starry-eyed knothole baseball campers.

As embarrassing as it continues to be, the Rose scandal has not been as damaging to baseball as the 1919 Black Sox scandal, primarily because the treachery committed involved a single person, not multiple members of one and possibly two teams. Nevertheless, it has bruised the game. After Bart Giamatti announced Rose's banishment back in 1989, he concluded his remarks on the case with the following summary:

> The matter of Mr. Rose is now closed. It will be debated and discussed. Let no one think it did not hurt baseball.

That hurt will pass, however, as the great glory of the game asserts itself and a resilient institution goes forward. Let it also be clear that no individual is superior to the game.

The accuracy of Giamatti's points have all been borne out, except for the first one. The Rose case is not closed, it is still hurting baseball, and it is a pain that apparently is never going to go away...until Rose dies or baseball somehow finds a way to give him what he wants most: a chance to gain election into the National Baseball Hall of Fame. It is clear that baseball has erected boundaries that Rose will never be allowed to cross: he will never be allowed to own or manage or work for any major league organization, in any capacity, on any level. But it is difficult to see how Rose, notwithstanding his apparent continuing addiction to gambling and

## MARTY'S ONE UGLY MOMENT

Beloved Reds radio broadcaster Marty Brennaman is a class act and a Hall of Fame broadcaster to boot, but even Marty had an ugly moment in the booth. On April 30, 1988, umpire Dave Pallone made an indecisive call at first base that led to a Mets run and a heated protest from manager Pete Rose. During the nose-to-nose, wildly gesturing argument, Pallone accidentally poked Rose in the face. In response, Rose pushed Pallone twice with a forearm. Rather than try to defuse the situation, Brennaman, who prides himself on "calling them as he sees them," attacked Pallone, calling him incompetent and a "horrible umpire." Reds fans enjoy Brennaman so much that they often tune in his broadcasts even when they are in attendance at Reds home games, and Marty's comments had the potential of turning the argument into a riot at Riverfront Stadium. As it was, fans showered the field with debris and caused a 14-minute delay in the game. Brennaman was later summoned to New York by then-National League president Bart Giamatti and chastised for "inciting the unacceptable behavior of some of the fans" with "inflammatory and completely irresponsible remarks."

controversial remarks, could harm the game in any material way by joining its most exclusive fraternity. Unless, of course, Rose's election and subsequent presence were enough to cause a boycott of future Induction Weekends by current Hall of Famers unwilling to forgive and forget as so many fans are willing to do. The greatest tragedy for Rose is the very real possibility that his actions have caused a significant number of the greatest players in history—the men who are his only real peers in terms of achievement on the diamond—to conclude that as great a player as he was, Pete Rose does not have the character to be recognized as a Hall of Famer.

## SCANDAL IN THE OWNER'S BOX: MARGE SCHOTT

Former Reds owner Marge Schott is another person who, unfortunately, must be included in any review of the ugliest moments and behavior in team history. Cincinnatians were predisposed to like the chain-smoking, plain-talking Chevrolet dealer when she bought a majority interest in the team. After all, she was a local girl, a huge Reds fan, a grandmotherly type who smothered animals and kids with hugs and kisses, and a civic-minded person who could be generous to charities and public institutions, such as the Cincinnati Zoo. Marge also received credit for saving the franchise for Cincinnati, although there really was no danger of the team leaving town—a fact she never made any attempt to clarify. And as a woman trying to make it in the men's worlds of business and baseball, she had a large reservoir of goodwill to draw upon. The public was more than willing to overlook her obvious flaws, such as her egotistic self-promoting and her legendary penny-pinching, as colorful self-defense mechanisms. That is, until her more serious character flaws were exposed.

Marge Schott's world began to unravel when she fired Reds comptroller Tim Sabo, the only African American employee in the Reds front office during the Schott regime. Sabo, who like most Schott employees did not enjoy working under the oppressive, intimidating conditions that prevailed in Schott businesses, would have left quietly had Schott not tried to cheat him out of benefits that had been promised to him when he was hired. As it was, he felt he had no choice but to sue, and in so doing he charged that he had been wrongfully fired in the first place, simply because of his skin color. In the course of the legal battle between Sabo and Schott, witnesses to the slurs that Schott had been uttering for years—she referred to both Dave Parker and Eric Davis as "my million-dollar niggers"—finally went public, and the nation as well as the citizens of Cincinnati became aware of Schott's appalling racial bigotry. As it turned out, Schott was an equal-opportunity offender, and she managed to insult Jews, foreigners (particularly the Japanese), homosexuals, and just about any other group of people with a common identity. One memorable example of Schott's insensitivity was her failure to understand why Jewish front office employee Cal Levy was disturbed to find an armband decorated with a Nazi swastika at her home during a dinner party. As usual, when asked about the incident, Schott's explanation only got her into deeper trouble. "Hitler was good in the beginning. He just went too far," she said once she got onto the topic of Nazi uniforms. It also became clear that Schott was not just extremely frugal personally, but that she was greedy and often unfair, if not downright malevolent, in her financial dealings with employees, associates, and business contacts. In order to save a relative pittance, she heartlessly canceled the health insurance of loyal retired front office employees who had never made much money working for the Reds; she angered the entire scouting department by continuously challenging every routine minor expenditure of the scouts who spent most of their time on the road; and she improperly withheld profits that were owed to her ownership partners on the Reds. Even during her greatest moment as a baseball executive, the Reds' triumph in the 1990 World Series, which should have brought her generous instincts to the forefront, her cheapness intruded and put a damper on the celebration. Upset that the Reds did not clinch the Series in Cincinnati where she could have basked in the praise of happy Cincinnatians, Schott refused to arrange for a victory banquet at the Oakland hotel where the team was staying. Pathetically, some of the players made a run

**Owner Marge Schott's prejudiced views and penny-pinching ways squandered much of the city's goodwill, and she eventually sold the team in 1999.** (Photo courtesy of Getty Images.)

to a fast food joint and brought back hamburgers for the famished celebrants.

For her racially offensive remarks, baseball's executive council suspended Schott for one year on February 3, 1993, fined her, and ordered her to participate in a multicultural training program. The training did not take, though, and she was suspended again on June 12, 1996, through the end of the 1998 season. By that time, though, the public had just about lost patience with her, and the incident that caused many fans to lose all respect for her occurred on Opening Day 1996, when for the first time in major league baseball history an umpire collapsed and died on the diamond. Twenty-five-year umpiring veteran John McSherry died of a heart attack seven pitches into the game between the Reds and the Montreal Expos, and after the other three umpires, the managers, and the players discussed the situation, it was decided to postpone the game until the following day, when the two teams were scheduled to be off. This gesture of respect was fine with everyone but Schott, who could not believe the game was being postponed and whose comments sounded like the complaints of a spoiled child whose birthday picnic was rained out. "I feel cheated," she said. "This isn't supposed to happen to us, not to Cincinnati. This is our day. This is our history, our tradition, our team. Nobody feels worse than me."

Schott never did regain control of the Reds. In the fall of 1998 she was charged with falsifying records at her car dealership, and rather than face an indefinite suspension from baseball she decided to get out of baseball. On October 23 she signed an agreement obligating her to sell her interest in the ballclub, and the next spring on April 20, 1999, she sold her shares in the team to a new ownership group headed by Cincinnati financier Carl Lindner. From that time until her death on March 2, 2004, she stayed out of the limelight and out of trouble. Hundreds of people visited the funeral home to pay their respects, and invariably they preferred to remember the good things about her life, especially her generosity toward numerous good causes. Former baseball commissioner Fay Vincent's remembrance of her was an honest attempt to assess her impact on the game, expressed as kindly as possible: "I guess I always thought of her as a tragic figure. I think she tried very hard to do the right thing for baseball, but she had some enormous limitations and she had some difficulty in overcoming them."

## THE REDS PITCHER WITH NO (SELF) CONTROL

Former Reds relief pitcher Rob Dibble was the ugliest-acting Reds player by far. For a time, Dibble was a great pitcher and could have landed in the Hall of Fame if he could have kept up his phenomenal pitching; when it came to his behavior, it's a miracle he never landed in jail!

The Reds drafted Dibble out of Florida Southern College in 1983, and Rob began his minor league career as a starting pitcher. He got everyone's attention when he moved to the bullpen and struck out 73 batters in 65 innings for Cedar Rapids in 1985. After dominating American Association batters for Nashville, Dibble got called up to the Reds halfway though the 1988 season. If anything, he was even better in the major leagues, whiffing exactly a batter an inning in 59 innings, compiling a 1.82 ERA, and holding National League hitters to a .207 average. The next year Dibs established himself as one of the best relief pitchers in the game. He went 10–5 with a 2.09 ERA and set a new major league record for strikeout ratio—12.8 per nine innings. In 1990 Dibble lowered his ERA to 1.74, and in 1991 when he switched from setup man to closer he saved 31 games and broke his own strikeout ratio record by whiffing batters at a rate of 13.6 per nine innings. He was elected to two NL All-Star teams and was voted co-MVP (with fellow "Nasty Boy," Randy Myers) of the 1990 NLCS. With a fastball that sometimes reached 100 mph, the 6'4" 230-pound Dibble

**Reliever Rob Dibble was a Nasty Boy on—and at times, off—the field for the Reds in the late 1980s and early '90s.** (Photo courtesy of Mike Shannon.)

was the most intimidating pitcher to ever wear a Reds uniform; however, manager Pete Rose could see from the beginning that the big right-hander's delivery put an excessive amount of strain on his arm, and shoulder injuries did in fact end his career prematurely. Perhaps that's just as well, since a longer career would have given Dibble a chance to get himself thrown out of the game for acting like...well, an idiot, if the truth be told.

In a career that lasted six and a half years, Dibble was suspended by the National League five times for a total of 17 games. His record of mayhem-instigating on the diamond is something any masked professional wrestler would be proud of. Here is the path that Hurricane Rob took through baseball:

1987—While pitching for the Nashville Sounds, Dibble threw a ball over the roof of the stadium and into the parking lot. Fortunately, the baseball meteor hit no one. In a different game he was thrown out by the umpire after he hit the batter with a pitch. Dibble's manager jumped on his back in an effort to restrain him, but the enraged Dibble flung the manager off. It took three teammates to pull him away from the umpire. Finally, while warming up in a third game, he fired his first four pitches into the Sounds' dugout and the fifth one off the press box window.

March 23, 1989—After giving up a game-winning home run in a spring exhibition game, Dibble pitched a fit, pounding the clubhouse wall with a bat, turning over a couple of picnic tables, and tossing some metal folding chairs into a pond.

May 23, 1989—After the Cardinals' Terry Pendleton drove in a run against him, Dibble picked up Pendleton's bat and flung it halfway up the screen in front of the grandstand.

July 8, 1989—Dibble set off a brawl between the Reds and the Mets in New York by nailing Mets second baseman Tim Teufel in the back, a hit-by-pitch ruled intentional by the home plate umpire. Teufel charged the mound and slugged Dibble upside the head. The two players were momentarily separated but broke free and went at it again. After the game, security personnel had to intervene to keep players on the two teams from starting the fight again in the runway connecting the home and visitors' clubhouses.

April 11, 1991—Dibble infuriated the Houston Astros and started another brawl by throwing a pitch behind the head of shortstop Eric Yelding. (Throwing behind the head of a batter is considered to be more dangerous than throwing at him because a batter's instinct is to move his head backwards.) The Astros were so mad at Dibble that one of them stole his glove during the melee and never returned it.

April 28, 1991—In a fit of pique after struggling to close out the Reds' 4–3 win over the Cubs at Riverfront Stadium, Dibble hurled the game ball more than 400 feet into the center-field stands where it struck and injured a grade-school teacher. Fortunately for Dibble, the young lady let him off with the payment of her medical bills. The National League, on the other hand, leveled its second fine against the out-of-control pitcher.

July 23, 1991—In one of the ugliest displays of poor sportsmanship ever seen in the major leagues, Dibble retaliated against Doug Dascenzo's successful suicide squeeze bunt by throwing at the legs of the Cubs out-fielder as he ran to first. The National League fined Dibble but spared him the suspension he deserved when he agreed to undergo counseling.

June 24, 1992—Dibble didn't start the donnybrook between the Reds and Astros that took place on this date, but he raced out of the dugout to attack Houston pitcher Pete Harnisch, who'd just thrown a pitch behind the Reds' Reggie Sanders. Astros coach Ed Ott, known in baseball as somebody you don't mess with, got Dibble in a choke hold and almost squeezed the life out of him. Result: another four-day suspension for Dibble.

August 30, 1992—Another postgame explosion by Dibble after he served up a game-losing three-run homer to the Mets' Bobby Bonilla. On national television, Rob ripped the buttons off his throwback 1962 Reds jersey as he left the field and then did $1,600 worth of damage to the visitors' clubhouse at Shea Stadium.

September 17, 1992—Dibble got into a fight with his own manager, Lou Piniella, after a 3–2 win over the Atlanta Braves. Dibble antagonized Piniella by contradicting Piniella's explanation to reporters about why the manager used Steve Foster in relief instead of Dibble. Before the game Dibble had told Piniella that he had a tight shoulder, but he told reporters afterward that his shoulder was fine.

Nobody ever figured out exactly what made Dibble, who seemed to be a nice guy away from baseball, such a crazy man in uniform, but it probably had something to do with his baseball persona. Dibble and bullpen buddies Randy Myers and Norm Charlton styled themselves the "Nasty Boys," and for Dibble the nastiness was not something he could confine to his pitches. The clearest insight Dibble ever provided into his psyche came when he gave some advice to San Diego Padres reliever Trevor Hoffman. Dibble described himself as having a "Black Knight mentality," and he told Hoffman to pitch as if he were angry about something. Whether the ugly shenanigans were necessary for Dibble or not, he finally seemed to get his emotions under control in 1993. Unfortunately, he lost his control on the mound, went on the disabled list with shoulder problems in September, and never pitched for the Reds again.

# REDS RAP SHEET

Considering the number of players who have played for the Reds over the years, the number of them who have run afoul of the law is extremely few. Pete Rose, who served two five-month concurrent sentences in federal prison in Marion, Illinois, for tax evasion, is the only Reds player to do hard time. Frank Robinson was arrested in 1961 on a concealed weapons charge, and some Cincinnatians believe that the incident was never forgotten and was a factor in Robinson's trade to Baltimore. Former Reds second baseman Johnny Temple had money problems in retirement, and his financial difficulties apparently led him into trouble. In 1977 he was arrested and charged with grand larceny in connection with the theft of heavy construction equipment. Outfielder Deion Sanders was arrested on August 8, 1994, in an incident that was as silly as it was criminal. When Sanders tried to drive his motor scooter out of Riverfront Stadium through a pedestrian exit, a police officer ordered him to stop and leave by a different exit. Sanders ignored the order, and as he drove past, the officer grabbed hold of him and was dragged about 20 feet. Sanders was charged with resisting arrest, failure to comply, and leaving the scene of an accident, but a jury exonerated him on all counts. Outfielder Ryan Freel's offenses were a little more serious. After Opening Day 2005, Freel was arrested in Bellevue, Kentucky, on a DUI charge. After he pled guilty, he was fined $600, had his driver's license suspended for 90 days, and was ordered to undergo alcohol evaluation and treatment. Less than a year later, Freel slipped up again, although thankfully he was not behind the wheel this time. He was arrested in a pool hall in Tampa, Florida, and charged with disorderly intoxication. Understandably embarrassed and not thinking clearly, Freel tried to conceal his identity as a baseball player, telling police, "I'm unemployed."

Although we regard those who commit it more as victims or lost souls than as criminals, suicide is against the law, and at least four Reds have died at their own hands. Morrie Rath, who played second base for the 1919 Reds, shot himself in 1945, as did Virgil Stallcup, who was the Reds regular shortstop from 1948 through 1951. The most heartrending Reds suicide occurred in the middle of the 1940 National League pennant race when backup catcher Willard Hershberger slit his throat with a razor in a Boston hotel bathroom while his teammates were playing a doubleheader. Hershberger was extremely well liked by his teammates and popular with Reds fans, but he blamed himself for a Reds loss and

# THE FANS AT THEIR UGLIEST

On the whole, Cincinnati's fans have been among the most knowledgeable, most loyal, and most gracious fans in baseball, but they've had their ugly moments they'd soon forget about if they could. Perhaps the ugliest thing Reds fans ever did was to literally boo Joe Nuxhall out of town. Joe had a bad season in 1960, compiling a 1–8 record with a career-worst ERA of 5.34. That was a hellish summer for old Hamilton Joe, for every time he stepped out of the dugout at Crosley Field, Reds fans let him have it. What Joe heard was not your run-of-the-mill booing either, but the most vicious, spiteful, uncalled-for abuse imaginable. Perhaps there was an element of jealousy in the fans' displeasure, and they took the opportunity of Nuxhall's poor performances to vent camouflaged expressions of envy. That seems to be the idea behind the explanation offered by sympathetic Reds catcher Ed Bailey, who said, "The fans were unmerciful. I'd never seen anything like it. Seemed like the Cincinnati fans were harder

**Reds great Joe Nuxhall poses with the statue erected in his honor outside of Great American Ball Park in 2003. The team's beloved announcer passed away in 2007.**

on their own—guys from that area—than they were on any of the rest of us. It was the same with Herm Wehmeier. The guy was a helluva pitcher and they booed him right out of town. Drove him crazy. I often thought that if he and Joe had played in another city, things might have been completely different."

The booing of Joe Nuxhall was so ugly that his wife, Donzetta, quit going to Reds games to watch him pitch, and so ugly that Powell Crosley, a normally hands-off owner, stepped in and decided to get Joe out of town for his own good and that of his family. When the Reds dealt Nuxhall to the Kansas City Athletics on January 26, 1961, for John Tsitouris and John Briggs, it was essentially a mercy trade. It also upset Nuxhall, who despite the treatment of the fans, still loved the Reds and wished to remain with the team. The Reds brought Nuxy back to town in July of 1962, and he finished out his career in Cincinnati. More important, Joe went on to have a long and distinguished career in the broadcasting booth alongside Marty Brennaman. He became as beloved a figure behind the microphone as he had been a reviled one on the mound. The club and the fans of Cincinnati made it up to him by erecting a bronze statue of him outside of the new Great American Ball Park. It was a very pretty ending to an ugly beginning. Sadly, Nuxhall passed away on November 16, 2007, after a battle with cancer at the age of 79.

sank into a deep depression. Reds manager Bill McKechnie learned too late that Hershberger had probably never gotten over the death of his father, who had also committed suicide when Hershy was a youngster. While not as well known as the Hershberger case, the death of Reds pitcher Benny Frey was also a sad story. Distraught over the end of his career, Frey poisoned himself with carbon monoxide in 1937.

Finally, a handful of Reds players have been victims of violence perpetrated by others as far back as 1878. That's when the Reds first star player in the National League, Charley Jones, was assaulted by a woman who claimed to be his wife. On a Cincinnati sidewalk, she attempted to blind the slugger by throwing cayenne pepper into his face. Jones bailed out the woman, whom he said was his live-in girlfriend, not his wife. Former Reds pitcher Howie Fox went into the bar business in San

Antonio, Texas, after he retired from baseball, and it cost him his life. He was killed trying to break up a knife fight in his tavern in 1955, at the age of 34. Pitchers Ted Davidson and Clay Carroll were both lucky to survive ugly domestic scenes. During spring training of 1967 Davidson was shot by his estranged wife, twice: once in the left side and once in the right shoulder. He recovered enough to return to the playing field in June. In 1985 at Carroll's home in Bradenton, Florida, his 26-year-old stepson went berserk, killing Carroll's wife and wounding Carroll and their 11-year-old son. Most tragic of all is what happened to 25-year-old Reds outfielder Dernell Stenson when he was playing for the Scottsdale Scorpions in the Arizona Fall league in 2003. During their theft of his SUV, four men kidnapped Stenson and then murdered him when he tried to escape. They riddled his body with bullets and then ran over it with his own vehicle. More than 30 of Stenson's Cincinnati and Arizona teammates, including Barry Larkin, Adam Dunn, and Ken Griffey Jr., attended his funeral in LaGrange, Georgia.

## BRAWLERS AND FIGHTERS

Reds players and teams have been involved in more fights and brawls than the ones instigated by Pete Rose and Rob Dibble. In fact, we could write an entire book on the subject and not cover them all. So let's content ourselves with a review of some of the more interesting ones.

Boston Braves coach Art Devlin once got into a fight at Redland Field that surely caused him afterward to ponder, "What was I thinking?" For some reason Devlin ragged Reds third baseman Babe Pinelli mercilessly for the first three innings of the game on July 25, 1926. As he jogged to his position in the top of the fourth, Pinelli bumped into Devlin on his way to the third base coaching box, whereupon Devlin punched Pinelli. Bad idea. Whether Devlin knew it or not, Pinelli had been a professional boxer in San Francisco, and he unloaded on the Boston coach, landing eight or nine hard punches before both benches emptied. This primed the players on both teams for more action, and it came later when Braves outfielder Jimmy Welsh tried to run over Reds catcher Val Picinich. Val punched Welsh in the nose, and both benches emptied again. This time it took the Cincinnati police to restore order. During the fracas, Boston outfielder Frank Wilson punched a police officer, and for that he was hauled off to the hoosegow, still wearing his uniform.

Pitcher Raul Sanchez had a career that lasted only 49 games in three seasons over an eight-year span, yet he managed to touch off two brawls while he was in a Reds uniform. The first one came on July 11, 1957, at Ebbets Field. In the fifth inning, the Dodgers' Jim Gilliam was trying to beat out a bunt down the first-base line when he collided with Sanchez attempting to field the ball. Sanchez and Gilliam started trading punches, which led to a wider brawl between the teams. The luckiest man on the field turned out to be Dodgers second baseman Charlie Neal, who clobbered Reds third baseman Don Hoak with a roundhouse punch when Hoak ran over to lend assistance to Sanchez. The pugnacious Hoak had been nicknamed "Tiger" by the same Brooklyn Dodgers when he'd played for them because of his penchant for fighting, but this time he was restrained before he could get his hands on Neal. Hoak promised to get revenge against Neal but never got the chance to exact it. Sanchez spent 1958 and 1959 in the minors but returned to the Reds in 1960. Before the game between the Reds and Philadelphia Phillies on May 15, he was told he was being sent back to the minors again. It was probably not a good idea to then send him into the game that night to pitch. Sure enough, the angry Sanchez hit three of four batters he faced at one point in the eighth inning, which caused Phillies manager Gene Mauch to run to the mound to attack Sanchez. This incited a complete war between the two teams, which went on for about 15 minutes. Two of the more notable fights were the ones between a pair of future Hall of Famers—Frank Robinson and Phillies pitcher Robin Roberts—and the one between 6'8", 225-pound Phillies pitcher Gene Conley, a pro basketball player, and the Reds mighty-mite second baseman Billy Martin, who stood 5'11" and weighed 165 pounds after a good meal. Martin, a skilled and dangerous fighter, didn't really harm Conley much, simply because he couldn't reach Conley's face.

# AND IN THIS CORNER...SECOND BASEMAN, BILLY MARTIN!

If anybody on the Reds out-Dibbled Dibble before Dibble, it was former Yankees second baseman Billy Martin, who came to Cincinnati after stints with the Indians, Tigers, and Kansas City A's. Martin, who came to town with a reputation as an instigator and a brawler, was with the Reds for only one season (1960), and true to form he did more damage with this fists than with his bat (with which he hit .246 with three home runs). Martin liked to drink and to hang out in bars, and his first altercation as a Red came in spring training. One day in Tampa after the Reds had worked out, Martin and outfielder Lee Walls visited a local watering hole. The bartender bought Martin and Walls a beer, which angered a local regular who complained that the bartender had never bought him a beer. Martin bought a beer for the disgruntled patron, who walked over to where Billy and Walls were sitting and threw the beer in Martin's face. One lightning-fast right hand from Martin and the unappreciative regular was lying on the floor, out cold. Billy had more luck—bad luck as it turned out—during a brawl against the Cubs on August 4. Martin had suffered a terrible injury with Cleveland while batting: he'd been hit squarely in the cheek by an errant fastball. He was still battling to overcome his plate shyness, and after Cubs pitcher Jim Brewer knocked him down with a high and tight fastball, Martin swung and missed at the next pitch. He let the bat slip out of his hands and sail past the mound on the first base side so that he could get close to Brewer as he walked out to retrieve it. Martin bent over, as if to pick up the bat, but then he raised up and decked Brewer with a solid punch to the jaw. A full-scale melee ensued, and Brewer was attacked and bloodied by a couple of other Reds players. Brewer suffered a fracture of the orbit bone around the right eye and sued Martin for $1 million. Although Cal McLish admitted that he'd been the one to deliver the damaging blow, Martin was the one blamed, and he settled the claim out of court six years later for about $25,000, which he paid out of his own pocket. The National League fined Martin $500 and suspended him five days for his role in the brawl, which helped seal forever Martin's somewhat undeserved reputation as a troublemaker and bully.

Later in that same season Frank Robinson got into another brawl-inciting fight with another future Hall of Famer, Milwaukee Braves third baseman Eddie Mathews. In the seventh inning of the first game of a doubleheader at Crosley Field, Mathews took exception to a hard slide by Robinson. The two players swapped punches, but Mathews clearly got the best of the fisticuffs, giving Robinson a bloody nose and a black eye. After the game Robby's eye almost swelled shut, yet he refused to sit out the second game. Instead, he practically beat the Braves single-handedly. He got on base four times, hit a home run and a double, and robbed Mathews of an extra-base hit with a great running catch, all of which earned him the respect and admiration of Mathews.

A few more of the worst brawls in Reds history, the main instigators, participants, and precipitating incidents:

- July 2, 1961, in Milwaukee—A 10-minute donnybrook starts after Reds pitcher Jim O'Toole barges into Ed Mathews in a rundown.
- July 3, 1967, in St. Louis—Cards pitcher Bob Gibson knocks Tony Perez down, causing a 12-minute melee. More than a dozen Reds suffer minor injuries.
- July 14, 1974, in Pittsburgh—The Reds' Jack Billingham hits Pirates pitcher Bruce Kison in retaliation for a Kison beanball, igniting the brawl during which Reds reliever Pedro Borbon bites Pirates pitcher Daryl Patterson. A Pirates broadcaster dubs Borbon "Dracula."
- May 25, 1979, in Los Angeles—Reds pitcher Dave Tomlin throws four consecutive pitches over the head of Davey Lopes because Lopes earlier hit a home run on a 3–0 pitch with the Dodgers already winning, 14–2.
- July 4, 1979, in Cincinnati—After a swap of beanballs, the whole Houston bench charges out to attack Reds third baseman Ray Knight, who'd been mouthing off to them.
- May 31, 1982, in Philadelphia—After Reds pitcher Mario Soto drills Bob Dernier and Mike Schmidt, he is hit with a pitch thrown by the Phillies' Ron Reed.

- May 27, 1984, in Chicago—Soto goes berserk over a foul ball, which is at first ruled a Cubs home run. He incites a brawl and is ejected even though the call is reversed.
- June 16, 1984, in Atlanta—Mad about a Claudell Washington home run, Soto throws at him in his next at-bat. In his third at-bat, Washington lets the bat fly toward Soto. Soto throws the baseball at the approaching Washington but hits umpire Lanny Harris and Braves coach Joe Pignatano, trying to intervene, instead.
- July 22, 1986, in Cincinnati—After Eric Davis slides hard into third, Mets third baseman Ray Knight pops him in the face with a right cross.

An altercation between the Reds' Eric Davis and New York's Ray Knight led to a full-fledged brawl in 1986.

- July 20, 1990, in Cincinnati—Reds pitcher Norm Charlton charges the mound and tackles Phillies pitcher Dennis Cook after Cook hits him in the leg.
- September 5, 1995, in Houston—Brushbacks and two HBP by the Reds' Xavier Hernandez led to an argument at home plate between the Reds' Ron Gant and Astros catcher Pat Borders, which Gant punctuates with a punch to the head of Borders.

# IN THE CLUTCH

B ill James, a tall, bearded Kansan with glasses, is the smartest person in the world—make that the universe—on the subject of baseball statistics. Clutch hitting is kind of a complicated subject—at least it can be when guys like Mr. James wrap their brains around it—and we don't need to get into the calculus and algebraic convolutedness of it here. Suffice it to say that Bill is skeptical that clutch ability, especially clutch hitting, exists in baseball. It is sufficient to also say that as far as Cincinnati Reds fans are concerned, we know that Bill James is *wrong!* Reds history is replete with instances of Redleg players coming through in do-or-die, make-or-break, and everything-on-the-line situations, and we prefer to attribute the spectacular, spine-tingling, crowd-electrifying results to their ability, desire, and sheer will to win and to come through for us, the fans, when it matters most.

## TAKE THAT, METS FANS!

The first name that comes to mind when the topic is clutch performances has to be none other than that of Pete Rose, the man who played on the winning team more times than any other player in baseball history. Rose was never described as a "five-tool player," yet he found as many different ways to beat the opposition as anybody else ever did, and he was always at his best when the game was on the line. For example, Rose once scored the winning run for the Reds on a passed ball...from second base; in another game, against San Francisco, he drove in the winning run by slapping a single down the third-base line on a 3–0 count when Giants pitcher Ron Bryant was trying to intentionally walk him; and he preserved more than a few Reds wins with outstanding catches in the outfield. And who will ever forget Rose's return to Cincinnati as a player/manager, when in his first at-bat he lined a hit into center field and, as the ball skipped past the Cubs' Bob Dernier, continued around second and into third base with his patented head-first slide? Or the 1970 All-Star Game, when Rose ran over catcher Ray Fosse to score the winning run? Although the play caused a shoulder injury that bothered Fosse for the rest of his career, the violent collision at home plate was for Rose simply an unintentional by-product of the way he felt baseball should be

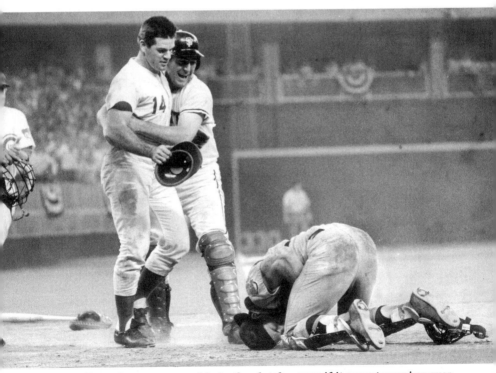

Pete Rose always came up big in the clutch—even if it meant running over Cleveland's Ray Fosse in the 1970 All-Star Game.

played. Asked after the game about his decision to plow through Fosse in order to touch the plate, Rose said, "I play to win. Period."

Rose won three National League batting titles, and in two of those years the race for the crown came down to the very end of the season. In 1968, Rose was running neck-and-neck with the Pirates' Matty Alou. On the next-to-last day of the season Alou went 4-for-4, but Rose upped him one by going 5-for-5—talk about clutch!—to pull ahead by one percentage point. (Rose, by the way, holds the NL record for collecting five or more hits in a game 10 times.) Rose took the title (.335 to .332 ) the next day by going 1-for-3, while Alou went hitless. Heading into his final at-bat of the following season, Rose was ahead of the great Roberto Clemente by the slimmest of margins: .0008 points. Rose captured his second straight batting title by beating out a bunt single. Rose also used his bunting ability to keep alive his 44-game hitting streak in 1978; hitless and down to his last at-bat in the 32nd game of the streak, Rose bunted safely against the Phillies' Ron Reed in the ninth inning.

And although Rose was not a home-run hitter, he did slam the ball out of the park on several occasions to win the Reds a ballgame. One such home run, which he knocked in October, was the most clutch of all the 4,342 hits (including postseason) Pete Rose collected in his long major league career.

Back in 1973, when the Reds and the New York Mets met in the National League Championship Series to see which team would advance to the World Series, the playoffs (as they were commonly called) were a single-round, best-of-five-games affair. The pressure in such a short series was much more intense than it is in today's expanded and longer-series format. On paper the '73 NLCS was a mismatch, pitting as it did the experienced, heavy-hitting Reds (who had represented the National League in the World Series two of the three previous years) against a Mets squad that had barely won the East Division with a humdrum record barely over .500 (82–79). The Reds went into the playoffs confident that they would smoke the Mets. As it turned out, the Series was a case of Goliath meeting David in the form of the Mets superb pitching staff. The Mets' pitchers held Reds hitters to a .186 batting average and limited Cincinnati to eight runs in five games.

The Reds won Games 1 and 4, and Pete Rose (who led all batters on both teams with eight hits and a .381 average) was instrumental in both victories. In Game 1, Tom Seaver shut the Reds out until Rose homered in the eighth inning to tie the game 1–1; Johnny Bench's homer in the bottom of the ninth won it for Cincinnati 2–1. The Mets knotted the Series 1–1 the next day when Jon Matlack fired a two-hit shutout against the Reds. The Series moved to New York for Game 3, and even though the Mets coasted to a 9–2 win, the game featured one of most explosive incidents, with Rose at its center, in the history of the postseason.

Rose came to bat in the fifth inning in a foul mood. The Reds were losing 9–2 (the final score of the game), and in Pete's previous time at bat the Mets fireballing Jerry Koosman had retired him on a slow curveball. Stepping back into the dugout Rose had screamed, "Throw the ball, you big dumb f*cking donkey!" The insult angered Koosman, who years later told writer Peter Golenbock that he walked Rose in the fifth because he threw four fastballs trying to hit Rose, but failed. Now also mad about having been thrown at, Rose slid hard into Mets shortstop Bud Harrelson while trying to break up a double play. Harrelson took exception to the flying elbow delivered by Rose as he executed his stand-up slide. He called Rose a dirty name and then threw a punch at him. Rose quickly pinned the slightly built Harrelson to the ground—Rose later claimed he never threw a punch at Harrelson—while Harrelson's infield partners came to his aid. Players from both

## DID YOU KNOW...

That the seats in the upper deck at Riverfront Stadium were red in color? Thus, a long ball that reached these distant seats was called a "red-seat" home run or a "red-seater." Powerful George Foster hit more red-seat home runs than anyone else (six).

benches and bullpens stormed the field and jostled each other while the fight between Rose and Harrelson was broken up. As coach Ted Kluszewski and catcher Johnny Bench pulled Rose away from the mob of Mets players, the main fighting took place between Reds reliever Pedro Borbon and Mets pitcher Buzz Capra. When things settled down and Borbon was leaving the field, it was pointed out to Pedro that he had accidentally placed Capra's Mets cap atop his head. Adding to his legend as a first-class flake, Borbon snatched the symbol of the enemy from his head and amazingly took a bite out of the bill of the cap.

**Never one to shy away from a fight, Pete Rose confronted the Mets' Bud Harrelson at second base during the 1973 NLCS. Rose and the Reds were eventually pulled off the field for their own safety after fans began throwing debris onto the field.**

When Rose took his position in left field, the rowdy New York fans began firing a shower of garbage down upon him. After a glass whiskey bottle whistled past Rose's head, manager Sparky Anderson pulled Rose and the rest of the Reds off the field for their safety. "Pete Rose has done too much for baseball to die in left field in Shea Stadium," he said. The game might have been forfeited by the Mets had New York manager Yogi Berra not been able to restrain the crowd through the intercession of Willie Mays, Seaver, Cleon Jones, and Rusty Staub, who appealed, successfully, for calm.

From that moment on, Pete Rose became the devil incarnate to New York Mets fans. It was suggested that Rose shake hands with Harrelson before the next game as a gesture of reconciliation, but Rose would not hear of it. "I'm not a little girl out there," he said. "My job is to break up the double play, to knock over the shortstop, to help my team win. That's what good fans expect me to do." Mets fans rained down a torrent of verbal abuse and insult on him throughout Game 4, and at one point a New Yorker even drenched him in a beer shower. Rose had the last laugh, though.

With Game 4 tied 1–1 in the top of the twelfth and the entire stadium booing his every move, Rose jacked one of reliever Harry Parker's pitches over the right-field fence to put the Reds up 2–1. The clutch home run was the ultimate retaliation for the way Rose was being treated by Mets fans, and to rub it in, to make good and sure every Mets fan in the ballpark could sense his disdain for them as well as his steely determination to trump their hatred of him, he ran all the way around the bases with his right fist raised in a gesture of triumph. To complete the vindication, it was the crazy Borbon who came on to set down the Mets in the bottom of the inning, making Rose's home run stand up as the game winner.

Unfortunately for the Reds, the Mets won the rubber game in Game 5 and sent the Reds home for the winter. That hurt Rose, but he was able to take some satisfaction in the most avenging hit of his career; a big home run by the game's most prolific singles hitter that was neither forgotten nor forgiven. A poster of the fist-wielding Rose rounding the bases was produced and became popular all over Reds country, while Mets fans renewed their abhorrence of the big bully with vociferous booing every time he set foot onto the diamond at Shea Stadium for the rest of his career.

## JOHNNY'S PARTING GIFT

If any other Reds player was as clutch as Pete Rose, it was Hall of Fame catcher Johnny Lee Bench. The team leader in grand slams (11) and postseason home runs (10), Bench definitely had a higher gear to shift into when the situation called for it. The game that first earned Bench widespread recognition for his clutch ability came on October 11, 1972, when the Reds and the Pittsburgh Pirates were locked in a struggle for the National League pennant. Entering the bottom of the ninth inning, the Reds trailed Game 5 of the NLCS 3–2. To finish off the Reds, Pirates manager Bill Virdon brought in his ace reliever, Dave Giusti, who'd saved 22 games during the regular season while fashioning an ERA of 1.93. Giusti only needed to get three outs and the Pirates would be National League champions.

Bench led off that fateful inning for the Reds, and right before he walked up to the plate, his mother Katy Bench called him over to the box seats. What did Mom want at this crucial point, not only in the life of her son, but in the baseball rooting lives of the 41,000 Reds fans screaming their lungs out for a rally? Nothing much...just a request for Johnny to please hit a home run. Amazingly, that is exactly what Bench did. After Giusti worked the count to 1–2, he threw a sinker on the outside part of the plate. Bench swung, connected solidly, and drove the ball far into the right-field bleachers for a game-tying, season-saving home run. The homer rattled Giusti and his reliever, Bob Moose, who five batters later wild-pitched home the winning run that gave the Reds the 1972 National League pennant. While George Foster scored that winning run, it was Bench who clearly was the hero. Afterward in the noisy Cincinnati locker room amid the celebrating Reds, hitting coach Ted Kluszewski marveled at what Bench had done: "I don't know of any other right-handed hitter in the league who has the strength to blast an outside pitch like that into the right-field seats. You have to be tremendously strong to go with an outside pitch and drive it almost 400 feet."

Of course there were many other clutch moments for Bench, including almost the entire 1976 World Series, when Johnny manhandled New York Yankees pitching (.533 with two home runs and 6 RBIs) to win the Series MVP trophy. But his greatest clutch performance came at the end of his career on September 17, 1983, when the Reds held a party to celebrate his retirement from baseball. A sellout crowd of 53,790 jammed into Riverfront Stadium to say good-bye to the last member of the Big Red Machine still with the team, among them a long string of celebrities and old friends who were there to congratulate Bench on the field prior to the game. As Bench made a dramatic entrance that evening, walking through a door in the center-field wall and down a red carpet to a stage set up in the infield, the crowd gave

**Catcher Johnny Bench was never more clutch than he was during the 1976 World Series.**

him a standing ovation that lasted several minutes, and Bench waved his cap and blew giant kisses toward every part of the Stadium. After his accomplishments were enumerated and praised, he was showered with gifts, including a wheelbarrow full of golf balls—one for each of his career home runs—a fishing boat, a sterling silver plate designed with his uniform No. 5 set in rubies, a golfing trip to Scotland, and a new Ford Bronco.

When that was finished, Bench delivered his own short but heartfelt speech of gratitude. "Thanks to my friends for taking the time to be here," he said. "I am here because I love you. I chose to stay in Cincinnati for one reason: I love the city. I love the fans, and I was fortunate to play for the Reds. It has been a labor of love. I've tried to be the best player I could be, and it was easier because you were in back of me. I am very lucky, honored, and grateful...and I am going to try like hell to play good for you tonight."

No one could have known how prophetic that last statement would be. The years and the physical beating a catcher endures had taken their toll on Bench, and he was no longer the Reds' regular backstop, nor the same great power hitter he had once been, for that matter, but on Johnny Bench Night it was only fitting that he start behind the plate. That in itself was a thrill for the fans and brought back many great memories. The Houston Astros started a rookie pitcher, Mike Madden, and he walked Johnny in the first inning, bringing a hail of boos from the disappointed fans. Things were different in the third when Bench came to bat again. With a runner on first and an 0–1 count, Madden threw Bench a fastball over the plate, and Johnny took a vicious cut at it, hitting a screaming line drive toward left. The liner was not very high, and for a moment it looked as if it would bounce off the wall, but at the last instant it cleared the left-field wall for a game-tying home run, the 389th—and what would be the final—homer of Bench's career. Reds fans went crazy at the miraculous home run, which Bench seemed to have conjured up through sheer willpower. Bench batted twice more and singled before he was ceremoniously removed from the game. The Astros wound up winning 4–3, but the thrills Bench had provided were so wonderful and memorable, nobody especially seemed to mind. In the end, it was the guest of honor, Johnny Bench, who gave the evening's lasting gift to Reds fans: another clutch hit in his long and eventful career.

# CONFIDENCE MEN

To play baseball well, you need confidence. You need to be drowning in it, if possible, because failure is a built-in component of the game. A hitter who bats .300, for instance, is accounted nifty with the stick, even though batting .300 means a failure rate of 70 percent! Major leaguers need that confidence just like high schoolers, and sometimes it is just as hard to come by for the pros as it is for the amateurs.

The 1961 Cincinnati Reds certainly had their struggles with confidence, as no one seemed to believe in them for the longest time. Especially not the so-called experts, who kept predicting that the Reds would fade down the stretch and be overtaken by a team more worthy of the National League pennant. The Los Angeles Dodgers were the team that most of the experts thought would eventually expose the Reds as pennant imposters. But as Reds fans know, the Dodgers never did catch the Reds in 1961, and the main reason they didn't is that two Reds starting pitchers turned in clutch performances on the same day of the season.

On August 15 the Reds opened a three-game series in Los Angeles, trailing the Dodgers by two games in the standings. If the Reds got swept, their pennant chances would suffer a serious, perhaps fatal, blow. The Dodgers came into the series hot, having won 19 of their previous 23 games. Now they were playing at home and had future Hall of Famer Sandy Koufax to throw against the Reds. Having such a pitcher on one's roster makes it very, very difficult for the opposition to pull off a sweep. But that is exactly what the Cinderella Reds did.

Joey Jay beat Koufax in the first game 5–2, as the Reds were helped by two base-running mistakes by the Dodgers. In the fourth inning Koufax lined a single into right field, but loafed down to first base and was thrown out by Frank Robinson. Later,

# CYCLE-HITTING REDS

To hit for the cycle means that a batter gets at least one single, one double, one triple, and one home run in the same game, not necessarily in that order. It's a pretty difficult thing to do, and most batters go through their entire careers without ever recording one. Eight Reds players have hit for the cycle, and the Reds king of hitting for the cycle is John "Long John" Reilly, who performed the trick three times...and twice within a seven-day period in 1883! Curiously, the first time Reilly hit for the cycle on September 12 he went 6-for-7, as did teammate Hick Carpenter. It was the first and second time a Reds player collected six hits in a game, and it remains the only time in baseball history that two players from the same team have gotten six hits in the same game. Besides Reilly, only two other players, Bob Meusel and Babe Herman, have hit for the cycle three times. Seven other Reds players have hit for the cycle, one time each:

- Bid McPhee, second baseman, 1887
- Tom Parrott, pitcher, 1894
- Mike Mitchell, outfielder, 1911
- Heinie Groh, third baseman, 1915
- Harry Craft, outfielder, 1940
- Frank Robinson, outfielder, 1959
- Eric Davis, outfielder, 1989

with the Dodgers trailing by three runs, Duke Snider tried to stretch a single into a double, and he was easily thrown out at second by center fielder Vada Pinson.

The next day 72,140 Dodgers fans, realizing the importance of the games, showed up for the doubleheader between the two contenders. This remains the largest crowd ever to watch the Cincinnati Reds play. Knuckleballer Bob Purkey was suffering from a sore arm, but he took the ball and shut down the Dodgers 6–0 on four hits in the first game. Jim O'Toole toed the slab for the Reds in the second game, and he did even better than Purkey, holding the Dodgers to two hits while also pitching a shutout, 8–0. The Dodgers had not been shut out in a doubleheader for 25 years, and it would be the last time the Reds ever pulled off the trick. What made the double shutout even more exceptional was the fact that Purkey and O'Toole held the Dodgers without a run for 18 consecutive innings in Memorial Coliseum, where the Dodgers were playing until their new ballpark, Dodger Stadium in Chavez Ravine, was ready. Memorial Coliseum was not a baseball park at all, but an immense stadium built for the 1932 Olympics. Converting it to baseball use had resulted in the ridiculous, batter-friendly dimensions of 251 feet down the left-field line and a scant 320 feet to the left-center power alley. A 40-foot-high screen had been installed on top of the left-field fence in an attempt to help the pitchers, but the bandbox was still a right-handed batter's dream.

The three-game sweep vaulted the Reds back into first place by one game, but more important it gave the club the tremendous boost of confidence it had been looking for. The Reds have never received a more clutch pair of pitching performances than those turned in that day by Purkey and O'Toole, because after that double shutout of the Dodgers, the 1961 Reds knew that they could do it, and they never relinquished first place again. As relief pitcher Jim Brosnan wrote in *Pennant Race,* the Cincinnati ballclub left Los Angeles having proved to themselves and to everyone else that "the Reds were for real."

## OLD COACH WILSON SHOWS THEM HOW IT'S DONE

When players don't listen to their coaches, the coaches often feel as if they'd like to get into the game and show the youngsters exactly how it's supposed to be done. Of course, the rules usually don't allow for such demonstrations, and the coaches are seldom young enough or skilled enough or in shape enough to play any longer. But once in a blue moon a coach gets such an opportunity, and it once happened with the Cincinnati Reds.

The 1940 Reds were a veteran team, determined to get back to the World Series and to make up for their loss to the New York

Yankees in the 1939 Series. The Reds were loaded with talent, especially at catcher. Heavy-hitting Ernie Lombardi, the only catcher besides the Reds' Bubbles Hargrave to win a batting title in modern National League history, was the first-string catcher, and he was ably backed up Willard Hershberger, another good hitter whom the Reds had acquired from the Yankees in late 1937. Hershberger was good enough to start on most any other team in the National League.

On August 3 the Reds' strength at the catching position began to dissolve when tragedy befell the team. Suffering from severe depression stemming from the notion that he had cost the Reds a victory by calling for the wrong pitches, Hershberger committed suicide in a Boston hotel while his teammates were at the ballpark playing a doubleheader. Hershberger had been popular with his teammates, and although his sad end cast a pall over the team, the Reds recovered and continued their quest for the pennant, promising to win a full share of World Series money for Hershey's mother back in California.

Things then got worse, when on September 15 Lombardi sprained his ankle so severely that he was finished for the season. This is where the hero of this story comes in. The Reds had two rookie catchers on the roster—Bill Baker and Dick West—and many assumed that one or both of them would strap on the tools of ignorance for the Reds. Manager Bill McKechnie had another idea: he turned to 40-year-old coach Jimmie Wilson, a former catcher for the Phillies and Cardinals, and asked him to do the job.

Wilson had a very good career as a backup major league catcher. He'd batted over .300 four times and had a lifetime average of .285. His baseball mind was so respected that the Phillies had brought him back from the Cardinals in 1934 to become their player/manager, a job he held through the 1938 season. The Phillies finished next-to-last three times and dead last twice during Wilson's tenure, but nobody blamed Wilson for the team's record, and in fact most observers marveled that he had gotten the woeful Philly clubs to play as well as they did. One clear indication of Wilson's acumen was his decision to transform the Phillies weak-hitting third baseman, Bucky Walters, into a pitcher—a change Reds fans would be ever grateful for.

Coming to Cincinnati in 1939 was like a reprieve for Wilson. "I'm tickled to death with my new job," he said. "But any job would be better than managing the Phillies." Although Wilson was signed as a coach, he let it be known that he could still do more than babysit the Reds players. "I feel I can catch some and will be ready whenever I'm needed," he said. After Lombardi went down, McKechnie took the veteran at his word and asked him to take over the Reds' catching duties. Wilson eagerly accepted the challenge and caught the Reds' final 16 games of the regular season in preparation for the looming World Series.

Hardly awed by the prospect of appearing on baseball's biggest stage since he had played in three World Series with the Cardinals, Wilson nevertheless was playing baseball's most physically demanding and most dangerous position. He was playing in an era that was downright prehistoric in its training methods and approaches to good health compared to what is available to players today. And in 1940, with life expectancies considerably lower than today, a 40-year-old professional baseball player seemed downright ancient.

None of this mattered to Wilson, who kept coming back to catch, day after day, after soaking tired and sore muscles for hours the night before.

So how did the 1940 World Series turn out for the Reds with the catching being done by an old coot who should have been coaching first base? Spectacularly!

The Reds beat the Detroit Tigers in a classic seven-game fight to the finish, and old-man Wilson played like a young stud. He batted .353 (second-highest average on the team) in six games; executed an important sacrifice bunt during the rally that led to the winning run in Game 7; and handled the pitching staff brilliantly, coaxing two wins from Paul Derringer after the Reds ace had failed to win his previous three World Series starts. And not only were the Tigers unable to run on his arm, but Wilson himself was credited with the only stolen base of the Series! The clutch performance was so inspiring that it prompted baseball commissioner Judge Kenesaw Mountain Landis to tell Wilson afterward in the Reds' happy clubhouse, "You've done our generation proud." The unsung hero of the 1940 World Series never played another game in the major leagues after Game 7. He went back to coaching, and in 1942, to no one's surprise, he was given another managerial job, this time with the Chicago Cubs. History has not recorded if he was ever tempted to put himself into the Cubs lineup in order to show the young bucks how it is supposed to be done.

## HATCHER'S HATCHET JOB ON A'S

When the Cincinnati Reds were preparing to meet the Oakland A's in the 1990 World Series, most people thought the A's would whip the Reds easily. They thought the Series would be a short one, maybe even ending in a sweep; it pitted a three-time championship ballclub (the A's) which had won 103 games in the regular season and swept Boston in the ALCS, against a group of inexperienced no-names, who had won 91 regular season games and had trouble getting past the Pirates in the NLCS. Well, the Series did last only four games, but it wasn't the A's who wielded the brooms. It was the Reds who did the sweeping, and Johnny Bench, working as a color man on national radio, was about the only voice in the land who predicted that the Reds would make such short work of the powerful A's.

Oakland seemed to have everything a great baseball team needs. They had power hitting in Mark McGwire (39 home runs), Jose Canseco (37), Rickey Henderson (28), and Dave Henderson (20); game-changing speed in leadoff man Rickey Henderson, who'd led the AL in stolen bases with 65; and a strong defense anchored by catcher Terry Steinbach and an airtight infield of McGwire, Willie Randolph, Walt Weiss, and Carney Lansford. They also had strong starting pitching—Bob Welch won 27 games, Dave Stewart 22, Scott Sanderson 17, and Mike Moore 13—and their bullpen was headed up by Hall of Fame closer Dennis Eckersley. To top it all off, future Hall of Fame manager Tony La Russa patrolled the dugout calling the shots for the A's.

What the experts and the A's, too, failed to take into account was that the Reds had some pretty good players of their own. After all, guys like Eric Davis, Barry Larkin, Chris Sabo, Hal Morris, Paul O'Neill, and Joe Oliver were all excellent players, and none of them were afraid of the A's. Better yet, the Reds' starting pitching, especially the trio of Jose Rijo, Danny Jackson, and Tom Browning, was every bit as good as that of the A's, and the Reds bullpen trio of Norm Charlton, Rob Dibble, and Randy Myers—the Nasty Boys—was lights out! In addition, Lou Piniella was no slouch as the Reds' skipper.

From the Reds' point of view, the two squads looked, at worst, evenly matched. Once the Series began, it became obvious that the Reds even had a secret weapon, a player who didn't get much attention from any quarter but who turned in one of the most astonishingly clutch performances in World Series history: journeyman outfielder Billy Hatcher.

The Reds acquired Hatcher right before the start of the 1990 season from the Pittsburgh Pirates. The 5'10" flyhawk with little power but good speed (53 stolen bases in 1987 for Houston) had broken into the major leagues with the Chicago Cubs and spent most of his career with the Astros. An injury to Eric Davis gave him a chance to play with the Reds in 1990, and he made the most of it, turning in his second-best season in the majors (.276 with 28 doubles and 30 stolen bases). The Reds were so satisfied with the play of Hatcher, who opened the season with an eight-game hitting streak, that when Davis came back off the disabled list, they left Billy in center and played Davis in left field. In their pre-Series scouting sessions, the A's didn't spend much time worrying about Hatcher, but they should have.

In the bottom of the first inning in Game 1, Hatcher, batting second in the Reds lineup, walked with one out and scored an out later when Eric Davis homered over the left-field wall to give Cincinnati a 2–0 lead. The homer by Davis off Oakland's ace Dave Stewart didn't demoralize the A's, but it did jack up the Reds and the crowd at Riverfront Stadium, who then believed more than ever before that the Reds were quite capable of pulling off what everybody else seemed to believe would be a huge upset.

**Billy Hatcher set World Series records and helped lead the Reds to an improbable victory over the A's in 1990.** (Photo courtesy of Getty Images.)

Billy Hatcher certainly played that way. He doubled and scored in both the third and fifth innings. He batted once more (in the sixth) and singled before the Reds closed out a 7–0 win. Hatcher went 3-for-3 with a walk and three runs scored. Amazingly, he was just getting warmed up.

In Game 2, won by the Reds in extra innings, 5–4, Hatcher doubled to left in the first, driving in Barry Larkin who had also doubled, and then scored on a ground-out. He doubled again in the third; bunted for a single in the fifth; tripled over right fielder Jose Canseco's head in the eighth; and was walked, intentionally, in the ninth. The 4-for-4 night gave him seven straight hits, which tied the record for consecutive hits in a World Series set by the Yankees' Thurman Munson in 1976. Hatcher had also reached base nine straight times, which set a new World Series record, and his five extra-base hits in consecutive World Series games tied another record.

The Series shifted to Oakland for Game 3, and Hatcher cooled off, batting only .400 (2-for-5), as the Reds won their third game in a row. By the time Game 4 rolled around, the desperate A's were sick of Billy Hatcher, and they found a way to take him out of the equation. After Larkin flied out to center to open the game, Dave Stewart threw inside and nailed Hatcher on the left hand. Hatcher stayed in the game and was caught stealing, but then left for the hospital where X-rays on his bruised hand proved negative. Even without their secret weapon, the Reds came through, eking out a 2–1 win that made them world champions. Many players contributed to the Reds victory—Jose Rijo was voted Series MVP—but nobody turned in a performance more clutch than Billy Hatcher. For the Series, Hatcher went 9-for-12 for a phenomenal .750 batting average, the best ever in World Series history. When asked after Game 2 about the records he had set or broken, Hatcher said he didn't much care about personal records. "I want a ring," he said. "When I was with Houston, Yogi Berra used to show me all those rings [Berra had earned with the Yankees], and I want one. They're pretty." The 1990 Reds got their rings, thanks in large part to Billy Hatcher.

## WORLD SERIES ACE: JACK BILLINGHAM

Jack Billingham is remembered most for his part in one of baseball's most historic moments: Hank Aaron's 714th home run. Aaron hit the homer, a three-run shot, at Riverfront Stadium on Opening Day 1974 on his first swing of the season. The point to note here is that Billingham found himself in a position to make history as Aaron's unintended accomplice because he had been chosen to start the opener, an honor traditionally reserved for the pitcher considered to be the ace of the pitching staff. And that was Billingham in 1973 and 1974 when he led the Reds staff in victories, 19 each year.

Billingham came to the Reds as part of the blockbuster trade with Houston at the end of 1971. Joe Morgan was the key to the deal, but getting Billingham was what swung the trade so clearly in the Reds favor. The contributions of the tall, blonde right-hander to the success of the Big Red Machine were easy to overlook because of his laidback personality and his methodical

# THE GREAT JERRY LYNCH

Jerry Lynch was not a great ballplayer, but he was a great pinch-hitter, who had his greatest season when it benefited the Reds the most.

A left-handed-hitting outfielder, Lynch was never a regular in the major leagues because there was no place to hide him on defense, besides the dugout. Considering how well he could swing the bat, he must have been truly terrible with the glove, an object he had little affinity with. He once borrowed the glove of Reds shortstop Alex Grammas, saying, "Maybe the glove will think I'm Alex and act accordingly." Grammas's glove wasn't fooled, and neither were the managers Lynch played for.

Yet Lynch was dangerous with a bat, very dangerous with the game on the line, and his ability to pinch-hit is what kept him in the major leagues. He broke in with the Pittsburgh Pirates in 1954, came to Cincinnati in 1957, and returned to Pittsburgh to close out his career after appearing in 22 games with the Reds in 1963. The most at-bats he had in one season was 420 in 1958, when he batted .312 for the Reds.

In 1961 Frank Robinson and Vada Pinson anchored the Reds outfield. Lynch competed for playing time in the remaining outfield spot with Wally Post and Gus Bell, both of whom wound up with more at-bats than Jerry. Yet Lynch's contribution to the Reds' pennant run was crucial. Manager Fred Hutchinson called on Lynch to pinch-hit 47 times in 1961, and Lynch came through 19 times for a .404 batting average. In addition, five of those hits were home runs, a total which tied Lynch for second most pinch-hit home runs in one season. Lynch's heroics in 1961 included pinch-hit home runs in back-to-back appearances on April 23 and April 26; two home runs, including a game-winning homer, hit on July 23 to help the Reds end a six-game losing streak; and a game-winning two-run homer hit on September 26 in the win that clinched a tie for the pennant. For the season Lynch batted .315 (his career high) with 13 home runs, 50 RBIs, and a .624 slugging percentage, all in only 181 at-bats.

Lynch currently ranks second in career pinch-hit home runs with 18 (behind Cliff Johnson, 20) and ninth in career pinch-hits with 116. His club record of 19 pinch-hits in one season (which he set in 1960 and tied in 1961) was broken in 2005 by Jacob Cruz (with 20), but his place in Reds history is assured. While he was not one of the big names on the Reds 1961 pennant-winning ballclub, he most definitely was a big man in the clutch.

style of pitching, but Billingham's importance can be grasped by comparing his record to that of the more stylish and sensational Don Gullett, usually accepted as the overall ace of the Big Red Machine. During their five seasons together on the Reds (1972–1976) Gullett won 70 games, while Billingham won 77.

Was Billingham any good in pressure situations? He was at his best in the World Series, which is baseball at its most pressurized. In fact, Billingham was almost unhittable during World Series play. In the three World Series he pitched in, "Easy Rider," as sportswriter Ritter Collett called him, struck out 19 and gave up only one earned run in 25⅓ innings for an ERA of 0.36, the all-time World Series record.

Billingham's best Series was his first against the Oakland A's. He started Game 3 and pitched eight scoreless innings to lead the Reds to a 1–0 victory. He pitched two-thirds of an inning in score-less relief to save Game 5, and he turned in a second good start in the crucial Game 7, giving up one run (unearned) in five innings. The 3–2 loss to the A's was hardly his fault.

Oddly enough, the final World Series start of Billingham's career came in Game 2 of the 1975 Series against Boston. The Red Sox got two runs off him in 5⅔ innings, including the only earned run ever scored upon him in World Series competition, but Billingham wound up with a no-decision. He also pitched, in relief, in Games 6 and 7 without being scored upon.

During the 1976 season Billingham was plagued by shoulder problems that had started in 1974, and he was demoted at one point to the Reds' bullpen. He went 12–10 on the year, and his 29 starts and 177 IP were his lowest figures to that point in his Reds career. Rookies Pat Zachry and Santo Alcala took up the slack in the Reds rotation during the season, and Zachry got the Game 3 start during the Reds' four-game sweep of the New York Yankees in the World Series that would have been reserved for Billingham had he been healthier. Billingham's only appearance against the Yankees came in Game 2 when he pitched 2⅔ innings of scoreless (of course) baseball in relief of Fred Norman.

Billingham wound down his career with the Detroit Tigers and Boston Red Sox. After he retired from pitching he ran a sporting goods business in Winter Park, Florida, and later served as a pitching coach for a team in the Florida State League. He was too humble to do so, but he could have introduced himself to young players who had never heard of him as "The Cincinnati Reds' Untouchable World Series Pitcher."

# IT AIN'T OVER 'TIL IT'S OVER

One of the great things about baseball is its impact on the American version of the English language. People who don't know the difference between the Metropolitan Sewer District and the New York Metropolitans of the National League use baseball expressions all the time, without even knowing it or giving a thought to where the expressions came from. The title of this chapter is such an expression, and it means that you are never supposed to give up prematurely. In other words, there is always hope for a successful or happy outcome until one runs out of time or chances or money or whatever it is that is needed to reach one's goal...or until, to use another common baseball expression, one is "mathematically eliminated." People who understand that "it ain't over 'til it's over" are often able to turn around unpromising situations. In baseball we call that kind of reversal a comeback. Like all of baseball's greatest franchises, the Reds have many interesting comeback stories. What follows are some of the best ones.

## KING OF THE REDS COMEBACKS

If "it ain't over 'til it's over" sounds a little Yogi Berra-ish, that's because the expression did originate with the former Yankees catcher, who has become famous for his unintentionally amusing, paradoxical verbal inventions. It was as the manager of the New York Mets that Yogi uttered the phrase in question, and he was trying to tell a pessimistic reporter not to count the Mets out of the 1973 pennant race in July even though the Mets were nine games out of first place. The Mets did go on to win the Eastern Division that summer, and coincidentally it was that same summer that the Cincinnati Reds made the biggest comeback in the history of their franchise.

Plagued by pitching woes, the defending National League champions struggled in the first part of 1973. After blowing a big lead in their June 30 game and losing it 8–7 in extra innings at home to the first-place Los Angeles Dodgers, the Reds found themselves in fourth place, with a 39–37 record, 11 games behind the Dodgers. It looked like the season was already over. The next afternoon, in the first game of a doubleheader, they were about to lose again and drop even further behind the Dodgers when third-string catcher Hal King was sent up to pinch hit against the Dodgers' Don Sutton with two on and two out, the Reds trailing 3–1. The Reds had acquired King and infielder Jim Driscoll in December of 1972 in a trade with the Texas Rangers and had recalled King from their Triple A farm club in Indianapolis just two weeks earlier.

Sutton worked the count to 2–2 on the left-handed King and then threw him a hanging screwball. King swung and deposited the ball over the right-field wall for a game-winning, walk-off three-run homer. A large welcoming committee of his teammates greeted King happily at home plate, and even though it was just one win, the dramatic come-from-behind nature of it galvanized the entire team. There was no Yogi Berra on the Reds to say it, but everybody all of a sudden had the feeling that the race for the Western Division pennant wasn't over until it was over. The Reds won the second game of the doubleheader, 3–2 in 10 innings— Tony Perez drove in the winning run with a single—and they beat the Dodgers again the following day, 4–2, on a two-run Perez home run in the bottom of the ninth inning. The Dodgers left town shaken, looking over their shoulders as they went. And well they should have, as the Reds staged the most remarkable comeback in team history. From July 1 to the end of the regular season, the Reds went 60–26. They caught L.A. on September 3 with a win in the Houston Astrodome and finished the season with a 99–63 record, good enough for a three-and-a-half game lead over the Dodgers, who finished in second place.

As for King, he batted only .186 on the season, but four of his eight hits were home runs. Three of those homers were of the pinch-hit variety, and the one he hit in the tenth inning on August 17 was another game-winning knock as it beat the Mets at Shea Stadium, 2–1. Unfortunately for the Reds, this story did not have a happy ending. By virtue of their superior pitching, Berra's Mets halted the Reds' march to the World Series by winning the 1973 NLCS three games to two. That defeat had its sting, but it took no luster off the accomplishment of the miraculous comeback of '73, led by King Hal of Cincinnati.

## THE 1975 WORLD SERIES: COMEBACKS x 4

The Reds can boast of one dynasty in the team's history, that of the Big Red Machine which held sway in the 1970s. As all Reds fans know, what certified the team as a contender to such a place of honor was the first world championship won by the Big Red Machine in 1975. That was the first time one of the rosters put together by GM Bob Howsam and managed by Sparky Anderson won it all, and until that happened the Reds were not going to be recognized as great, but merely as pretty darn good.

The 1975 World Series not only moved the Reds far down the path towards dynastic eminence, it also excited and captured the attention of the entire nation. Everybody, not just Reds and Boston Red Sox fans, seemed to discover and fall in love with baseball again, as that classic World Series enthralled all witnesses with its drama, poignancy, heroism, and the breathtaking skills of the participants. Obviously, since the Series went seven games, the Reds' defeat of the Red Sox, a most worthy adversary, was nowhere near a foregone conclusion. Yet many fans today, especially in light of the dynastic mantel draped around the team after its Sherman-like march through the 1976 postseason, do not remember how extremely close the 1975 Series was and how difficult it was for the Reds to finally prevail. This is best conveyed by the reminder that

---

# DID YOU KNOW...

That Sparky Anderson managed the Reds from 1970 to 1978 and is the winningest manager in team history? His given first name made him part of a tricky Reds trivia question: how many Georges were there on the 1975 Reds championship team? Answer: 4 (outfielder George Foster, coach George Scherger, outfielder George Kenneth Griffey, and manager George "Sparky" Anderson).

---

the Reds did not have to stage a comeback just to win Game 7; they needed comebacks in all four games they won! Without a huge portion of the good old "it ain't over 'til it's over" spirit to fortify them, the Reds might have been swept in the 1975 World Series!

The Series began in Boston on October 11 with the only game that would not involve at least one lead change. A pitching duel between Don Gullett and Luis Tiant disintegrated into a Boston cakewalk when the Red Sox scored all of their runs in the seventh inning to win 6–0. The Reds' first comeback came the following day. Flummoxed by Bill Lee's savvy and junkball pitches, the Reds trailed 2–1 going into the top of the ninth. A Johnny Bench double to open the inning led to Lee's replacement by Dick Drago, who retired the next two batters, bringing Boston to within one out of taking a commanding 2–0 lead in the Series. Two clutch hits—a single by Dave Concepcion and a double by Ken Griffey—put the Reds ahead 3–2; after Rawly Eastwick, who'd pitched a scoreless eighth, set the Sox down in order in the bottom of the ninth, the Reds had evened the Series.

Game 3 at Riverfront Stadium exhibited the seesaw, multiple-lead-change pattern that came to characterize the '75 Series. Boston scored first, in the second inning, but the Reds led 5–1 after five. Boston tied it up 5–5 with a pair of runs in the ninth, but the Reds came back to win it, 6–5, on Joe Morgan's bases-loaded single in the bottom of the tenth. The Reds' rally was punctuated by the Series's most controversial play. While sacrifice bunting Cesar Geronimo to second, Ed Armbrister hindered catcher Carlton Fisk, whose throw sailed into center field, allowing Geronimo to go to third and Armbrister to second. The Red Sox claimed Fisk was interfered with and demanded that Armbrister be ruled out. Plate umpire Larry Barnett denied the Boston appeal, after which Pete Rose was given an intentional pass, setting the stage for Morgan's game-winning single.

The Reds jumped ahead 2–0 in Game 4, but this time the Red Sox staged a rally and took the game by putting a five-spot on the scoreboard in the top of the fourth to win 5–4. Once again, in Game 5, Boston drew first blood in the opening frame on a triple by Denny Doyle and a sac fly by Carl Yastrzemski, but the resilient Reds tied it in the fourth, went ahead by one in the fifth, and put the game away with three runs in the sixth; the final score was 6–2.

Bad weather all across New England postponed Game 6 for three days, making anxiety-prone Sox fans more desperate than ever with their team one loss from elimination. With everything on the line, the game proved to be the most nerve-wracking, dramatic, draining, and exhilarating game imaginable. Boston came out with guns blazing and scored three big runs in the first inning. Cincinnati tied it up in the fifth on a walk by Armbrister, a single by Rose, a triple by Griffey, and another single by Bench. The Reds took the lead (but not control of the game) with two in the seventh and one in the eighth, but then former Red Bernie Carbo tied it up again with a sensational three-run pinch-hit home run into the center-field bleachers. It was Carbo's second pinch-hit home run of the Series. After the Reds went quietly in the ninth, the Red Sox loaded the bases with no outs in the bottom of the inning but failed to score. The Reds almost went ahead in the eleventh, but right fielder Dwight Evans made a spectacular leaping catch to rob Joe Morgan of a probable home run, and his throw back to the infield doubled Griffey off of first base. Finally, the issue was decided in an agonizing instant when Carlton Fisk led off the bottom of the twelfth. Pat Darcy, the Series-tying eighth pitcher used by the Reds in the game, had taken the mound for Cincinnati to start the bottom of the tenth inning. He had set down six straight Red Sox batters. On his second pitch of the twelfth inning Fisk hit a high fly ball that began curving foul down the left-field line. With Fisk frantically trying to wave the ball fair with both hands, it struck the foul pole for a game-winning home run, which sent all of New England into a state of bedlam and set up the seventh game showdown the next day.

For the sixth time in the Series the Red Sox scored first, with three runs in the third inning. Making his second start of the Series, Bill Lee held the Reds in check until the sixth when he threw Tony Perez one blooper pitch too many. Perez blasted the pitch over the Green Monster, Johnny Bench scoring ahead of him from second base, to cut Boston's lead to 3–2. An inning later after a blister forced Lee from the game, Rose singled in the tying run. In the ninth the Reds scored the game-winner by playing

Despite Carlton Fisk's home-run heroics, Pat Darcy (pitching) and the Reds took home the 1975 World Series trophy.

small ball: Griffey walked, went to second on a sacrifice, advanced to third on a groundout, and scored on Joe Morgan's bloop hit into center field. Much of the credit for the win was due to the Reds' often overlooked pitching staff, which, in the persons of Jack Billingham, Clay Carroll, and Will McEnaney, held Boston to one hit and no runs over the final five innings of the game, as the Reds offense slowly caught up and edged past the Red Sox.

When it was over, the 1975 World Series had exhausted everybody: the Reds, the Red Sox, and certainly the fans of both teams. With five-one run games, two extra-inning games, four games that were decided in the final inning, numerous lead changes, and five come-from-behind victories, including those four by the Reds, the Series could hardly have been any closer. It was highly appropriate that the Series-deciding hit produced by the Big Red Machine was not a tape-measure home run but a little dinker just past the infield. The never-say-die Reds had every right to claim that they were just like the investment firm that in television commercials of the time explained how they made their money. The 1975 Reds, in other words, could say that they had won the World Series the "old-fashioned way...we earned it!"

# THE RETREAD EXPERT

In addition to rousing comebacks by a team, baseball is also enlivened by personal comebacks in which a struggling individual player overcomes some kind of problem or adversity and returns to (or even surpasses) his former level of productivity. The Reds have always enjoyed their share of such comeback players, especially during the reign of general manager Jim Bowden, who was the master at finding players on the scrap heap who just needed a second chance to reclaim their careers.

After graduating from Rollins College (Florida) in 1983 with a degree in Business Administration and Communications, and aided by his knowledge of computers, Bowden landed a job with the Pittsburgh Pirates as the club's Assistant Director of Player Development and Scouting. In 1989 he worked for the New York Yankees as an assistant to the Senior Vice President–Baseball

Operations and was then hired by the Reds as an administrative assistant for both scouting and player development. In August of 1991 he was promoted to Director of Player Development, and in 1992 he was named Reds general manager, making him the youngest man (31) in baseball history to ever hold the position. Later that year he also assumed the duties of president and CEO when Marge Schott was suspended by Major League Baseball.

It was a meteoric rise to the top for Bowden, who most assuredly did not flame out once he got there. Bowden regularly did more with less (money, that is) than any of his counterparts. He was, in short, the perfect man for the job of running a big-league team in a small-market city. With his background in scouting and player development, Bowden knew what to look for. He was a keen judge of baseball talent, and most important of all he was not afraid to make daring moves he thought would improve the ballclub. The best example of that daring was his trade of the pitcher scheduled to be the Reds' Opening Day starter in 1998, Dave Burba, on the day before Opening Day! Not only did Reds fans not like the timing of the deal, they also did not care for the trade itself. Burba, after all, was regarded as the ace of the staff, and the Reds were not exactly stocked with great pitching. Worse, in return for Burba the Reds were getting from the Indians a young first baseman nobody had ever heard of. The trade turned out to be completely lopsided...in favor of the Reds, as the return for Burba was Sean Casey, the soon-to-be "Mayor of Riverfront," who quickly established himself as one of the Reds' best and most popular players.

If anything, Bowden was even craftier in signing free agents, especially those thought to be washed-up. Take Ron Gant, for example. The six-year veteran was released by the Atlanta Braves in February of 1994 after he'd broken his leg while riding on a dirt bike. Bowden took a chance on Gant, who sat out all of 1994 recuperating from the accident, and was handsomely rewarded by Gant's play in 1995. Gant made the National League All-Star team, and his 29 home runs and 88 RBIs in 119 games helped the Reds win the Central Division flag. Quite appropriately, Gant earned *The Sporting News*'s Comeback Player of the Year Award.

Given the Reds' historical difficulty in developing quality starting pitchers and the prohibitively expensive cost of signing star free-agent starters, Bowden was especially aggressive in trying to identify prematurely cast-off starting pitchers, to whom he gave second chances as if they were nothing more than Life Savers candy. One of the best examples of the presumed-to-be washed-up starting pitchers whom Bowden rescued was Pete Harnisch. Other general managers must have thought Bowden was crazy to waste his time on Harnisch, who not only had been through shoulder surgery, but had missed most of the 1997 season battling acute anxiety. The last thing most GMs want is a head case, but Harnisch overcame his bout with clinical depression to become the best starter on the Reds' roster. He was voted the winner of the team's Vander Meer Award (best pitcher) in 1998 and 1999, and his three-year total of 38 wins was the best such stretch turned in by a Reds pitcher since Jose Rijo won 44 games in 1991, 1992, and 1993. Bowden also signed Jeff Brantley in 1994 after the San Francisco Giants had dumped him, and Brantley responded by becoming a mainstay of the Reds bullpen. He capped his Reds career by winning the National League Rolaids Relief Man Award in 1996. Despite the dismal season Jeff Shaw turned in for the Montreal Expos and the Chicago White Sox in 1995, Bowden signed him as a free agent, and two years later Shaw won the Rolaids Relief Man Award as the Reds' closer.

Of course, not all of Bowden's gambles worked out. In 1995 he gave last chances to Jack Morris and Frank Viola, both one-time All-Star quality starters, but neither was able to recapture the effectiveness that had made them stars. These failures were relatively few and far between, though, and Bowden's penchant for giving cast-offs another look definitely helped the Reds deal with their budget limitations throughout his tenure with the ballclub. It was only fitting that after the Reds, unhappy that the team had not won a division title since 1995, dismissed Bowden in July of 2003, another franchise, the Washington Nationals, gave him a second chance of his own. Bowden remains at work with that ballclub, still as willing as ever to give baseball retreads a trial run.

# DOWN AND ALMOST OUT: THE COMEBACK OF JOSH HAMILTON

Drug abuse has done extensive damage to the game of baseball. It has wrecked the careers of too many players, some of them great talents, such as Darryl Strawberry and Dwight Gooden, who were on the way to the immortality of the Baseball Hall of Fame before they started taking drugs. Drug abuse has even led to the premature death of other players, such as Rod Scurry, Steve Howe, and Rod Beck. The Reds have fortunately experienced few problems with player drug abuse. Amazingly, the biggest gamble they have ever taken in trying to help a player resuscitate an expiring career was with a young man attempting a comeback from cocaine addiction. It doesn't get any riskier than that.

Coming out of Athens Drive High School in Raleigh, North Carolina, Josh Hamilton was the most talented prep baseball player in the country, with the credentials to prove it. Following his senior season in 1999, he was named USA Baseball's Amateur Player of the Year and *Baseball America*'s High School Player of the Year. He could do anything and everything on a baseball field, and do it with ease; the only question about his future in professional baseball was whether the team lucky enough to acquire his services should regard him as a hitter or a pitcher. That's because while he was a terrific hitter with loads of natural power, he had also pitched in high school and could throw the ball 96 mph.

In June of 1999, the Tampa Bay Devil Rays made Hamilton the first overall pick of the draft of first-year players, signing him to a $400,000 bonus. He was the 17th high school player to receive the honor and the first since the Seattle Mariners had taken Alex Rodriguez out of Westminister Christian High in Miami (Florida) in 1993. Hamilton's first four years in pro ball were a mixed bag. He performed brilliantly and consistently drew raves, won awards, and earned multiple recognitions as the top prospect in the leagues he played in, in the Devil Rays' organization, and even in the entire minor leagues; however, each year his season ended prematurely due to a variety of injuries. The injuries were not his big problem, though—it was the drug use, which started after he hurt his back in a truck accident on February 28, 2001, near his home in Bradenton, Florida.

When Hamilton began his pro career, his parents quit their jobs and lived with Josh wherever he went to play. His mother was driving the family pickup in Bradenton when a dump truck slammed into it. Josh suffered a back injury, and his mother had to be pried out of the truck. Shortly thereafter, she and Josh's father returned to North Carolina to continue her medical treatments. Bored because he wasn't well enough to play, alone for the first time in his life, and relatively rich, Hamilton started hanging around the Bradenton tattoo parlor where he had acquired several tattoos (much to the disappointment of his mother). He added more tattoos—he has 26 in all—and, worse, got sucked into the drug culture. Before long he was a drunk and a crack addict, and eventually, he says, he tried about every illegal substance to be found on the street.

Josh Hamilton had seemed like such a good kid—indeed he had always been a good kid—that no one really wanted to believe the rumors about him that began to circulate. Yet his erratic behavior made it clear that something was very wrong in the young man's life. After showing up late for workouts twice in one week during spring training of 2003, when he should have been fighting for a spot on the major league roster if not in the D-Rays' starting lineup, Hamilton was reassigned to the Devil Rays' minor league camp. Ten days later he disappeared. Six weeks later he showed up for workouts with Double A Orlando, insisting he had no drug problem, but he disappeared again nine days later. He wound up not playing at all in 2003, and in February of 2004 his drug abuse became public knowledge when Major League Baseball suspended him for 30 days. A suspension longer than 25 days meant two things: that he had failed two previous drug tests, and that the tests had detected his use of something harder than marijuana.

Hamilton's life continued to spiral out of control. He endured additional, lengthening suspensions, and as he later admitted he went through eight unsuccessful drug rehabilitation programs and attempted suicide at least three times. Realizing he needed help, Hamilton turned to Dean Chadwick, a Raleigh homebuilder and a recovering drug addict who testifies about the dangers of drugs before Christian groups. Hamilton stayed up one night talking until dawn with Chadwick who told him, "You get well or you die." Hamilton began dating Chadwick's daughter, Katie, and he and Katie later got married. But the marriage solved nothing. Hamilton remained hooked on crack, and even the birth of his daughter, Sierra, was not enough to cause him to reconcile with Katie after they inevitably became separated.

Hamilton hit bottom in October of 2005. With nowhere else to turn, he showed up—40 pounds underweight, half-dead, and coming off a crack binge—at his grandmother's house. Shocked as she was, his grandmother took him in and guided him toward sobriety, but not before he had a relapse and a pair of nightmares during which he dreamed of fighting against the devil. Tormented by his failure to subdue Satan in his first dream, Hamilton woke up at peace with himself after realizing through his second dream that Jesus Christ was always there beside him to help him vanquish the demons in his dreams and in his real life. Though his baptism would come later, Hamilton became a Christian at that moment and felt, for the first time in years, that he did have something to live for. He stopped using drugs on October 6, 2005; started working on being a better husband and father; and rededicated himself to fulfilling his potential as a baseball player, reasoning that God would never have blessed him with such extraordinary talent if He did not want Hamilton to make the most out of it.

Hamilton basically started over as a player. He stayed clean—people could see that he was a new man—and even though he hadn't played in a game in three years, his immense talent was still impossible to miss. On June 2, 2006, Major League Baseball granted him permission to participate in extended spring training with the Devil Rays, and at the end of the month he was given permission by MLB to participate in minor league games. He played in 15 games for the Hudson Valley Renegades of the NY-Penn League, the same Single A circuit he had played in during his rookie year (1999) as a professional.

Although the Devil Rays were still interested in seeing their investment in Hamilton pay off, they didn't think other clubs would be interested in a player with Josh's history. They left him unprotected and eligible to be drafted in the Rule 5 Draft. The night before that draft Reds GM Wayne Krivsky called manager Jerry Narron to ask, "What do you think of Josh Hamilton? We're thinking about drafting him." Narron, himself a native Tarheel whose brother Johnny had coached Hamilton when Josh was a teenager, was all for it. Said Narron, "My jaw dropped. I was so excited about it, knowing his history and knowing him personally. It just killed me to see the difficulties he had. But I want to give him every chance in the world to be successful and get his life back on track." In a prearranged deal, it was actually the Chicago Cubs who drafted Hamilton and then sold him to the Reds for $100,000. Much to the delight of Hamilton, who could hardly believe what was happening for him, the Reds opened spring training prepared to give him every chance to make the ballclub. They loved his talent and did not want to have to return him to the Devil Rays (along with $25,000), which is what they would be required to do if they did not keep him on the 25-man roster for the entire 2007 season.

Phenoms at spring training are as common a sight as old men wearing floppy fishing hats and chewing on cigars in the grandstand. Nevertheless, the way Josh Hamilton tore through spring training with the Reds in 2007 made everybody sit up and pay attention. Hamilton hit over .400 and played outfield like a Gold Glover. And his arm, which had always been rated exceptional, was still there. Reds fans knew this when they heard Marty Brennaman, the veteran of countless spring trainings who'd seen phenom after phenom come and go, get authentically excited describing one of Hamilton's long, powerful, and accurate throws from deep right field. When the Reds broke camp, Hamilton headed north with the team, and all of a sudden his incredible comeback was the biggest feel-good story in baseball. Hamilton made constant reference to Jesus Christ as his savior and insisted on giving the credit for his turnaround to God, but even skeptical members of the media were not put off by these blatant acknowledgments of religious faith.

As a recovering addict Hamilton knew that he could take nothing for granted. "I'm a drug addict," he said. "It's not terminal,

**Josh Hamilton emerged from years of drug abuse to become one of the feel-good stories of the 2007 season.** (Photo courtesy of Getty Images.)

but there is no cure. It's hell on earth. It's a constant struggle." He would be drug tested often, sometimes as often as three times a week, and one positive test would probably be enough to get him banned from the game for life. With no room for error the Reds took exceptional measures to help him. His old coach Johnny Narron, the Reds' video coordinator, became his companion on the road and even took charge of doling out Hamilton's meal money to him a few dollars at a time.

Opening Day is a huge deal for everyone in Cincinnati. Even veteran players can feel the unusual excitement in the air. Josh Hamilton, a recovering drug addict who'd played only 15 games in the low minors in the previous three years, could hardly believe he was standing on the turf of beautiful Great American Ball Park with his Reds teammates when the national anthem was played before the Reds' first game of the 2007 season on April 2. Hamilton did not start the game, but he came up to pinch hit for pitcher Kirk Saarloos in the eighth inning. The sellout crowd at GAB gave the rookie a 22-second standing ovation. When the noise quieted down, Cubs catcher Michael Barrett looked up at Hamilton and said, "You deserve it, Josh. Take it all in, brother. I'm happy for you." Hamilton hit the ball hard, to Cubs left fielder Matt Murton, who retired him on a sliding catch. The crowd gave him another ovation. On April 10 Hamilton made his first start, against the Arizona Diamondbacks, and he hit the first home run of his career off Edgar Gonzalez. The next day he homered again, and he continued to play so well that by the end of April he was named National League Rookie of the Month.

In late May, Hamilton went on the 15-day disabled list with a bad case of gastroenteritis. He was not surprised at all when doubters began to whisper about a drug relapse. He realized that such doubts would come with the territory, just as heckling from opposing fans did. In a six-game rehab stint with Triple A Louisville, he batted .333 with four home runs and six RBIs before being recalled to Cincinnati. Then on July 12 he went on the DL again, this time because of a sprained right wrist. At the time he had a .279 batting average with 11 doubles, 14 home runs, 30 RBIs, and a team-high slugging percentage of .543.

Toward the end of this second stint on the DL, Hamilton again suited up for a few games with Louisville to gradually work his way back into major league playing condition. He returned to Cincinnati so that he and his wife could host a special promotion at Great American Ball Park in conjunction with the Reds' game against the Padres on August 10: Josh Hamilton "Believe" Bracelet Night. The red cloth bracelets with the word "Believe" and Josh's No. 33 on them were given away to the first 20,000 fans to enter the ballpark, and after the game the fans were treated to a concert by the Christian rock band Mercy Me.

None of the ads promoting the event explained exactly what or who it was that people were supposed to believe in, but it really didn't need to be spelled out for them. Josh Hamilton had finally put his trust in God and been saved. It was only natural for him to want to share his faith with others. He also realized that as a major league baseball player he was a tangible, irresistible beacon

# HALL OF FAMERS WHO SPENT PART OF THEIR CAREERS WITH THE REDS

The list of Hall of Fame players who spent part of their careers with the Reds is pretty long. Unfortunately, most of the following players spent a very small part of their careers with the Reds. Typical was the case of pitcher Dazzy Vance, whom the Reds acquired near the end of his career. Vance went 0–2 with a 7.50 ERA in six games for the Reds in 1934 before the club sold him on down the road to St. Louis. The player on this list who contributed the most to the Reds was probably first baseman Jake Beckley. "Old Eagle Eye," as Beckley was called, came to the Reds during his 10th season in the majors, yet he was with the club for six-plus years, batting over .300 every season except one, with a high of .341 in 1900. Luckily for the Reds, the case of Sam Crawford, whom the Reds had at the beginning of his career, was atypical. It wasn't that the Reds didn't appreciate the talents of Crawford, who played four years in Cincinnati, batting at .330 and .333 clips his final two seasons. The Reds lost Crawford in a contract dispute to Detroit and watched glumly as he racked up another 2,466 hits for the Tigers.

This list brings up an interesting point; namely, the difficulty faced (even by the Hall of Fame) in assigning a player to a team when that player "distinguishes himself with multiple organizations." For example, the Hall of Fame assigns Frank Robinson to the Reds in a chart of Hall of Famers by team that is annually part of the "Around the Horn" News & Notes handout given to members of the media, even though Robinson himself chose to appear on his Hall of Fame plaque wearing a Baltimore Orioles cap. In making up the chart, the deciding factor for position players (such as Frank Robby) used by the Hall of Fame was games played. Reds fans certainly consider Robinson one of their own, and so he is left out of the list below.

| | |
|---|---|
| Jake Beckley | Kiki Cuyler |
| Jim Bottomley | Buck Ewing |
| Mordecai "Three Finger" Brown | Clark Griffith |
| Sam Crawford | Chick Hafey |
| Candy Cummings | Jesse Haines |

| | |
|---|---|
| Harry Heilmann | Tom Seaver |
| Miller Huggins | Al Simmons |
| Joe Kelley | Joe Tinker |
| George Kelly | Dazzy Vance |
| Mike "King" Kelly | Lloyd Waner |
| Rube Marquard | George Wright |
| Charles Radbourn | Harry Wright |
| Amos Rusie | |

of light that other people who were also fighting demons of their own were drawn to. It was fine with Hamilton, in other words, for people to believe in him, as long as that belief led to a strengthened belief in God. He perfectly understood why all sorts of people, but especially mothers and fathers, wanted to tell him about the people close to them who were also suffering. "They know where I've been," Josh said in a story that appeared in *ESPN The Magazine.* "They look to me because I'm proof that hope is never lost."

## THE REDS' BLOWN PENNANT

The 1964 Philadelphia Phillies live in infamy as some of the biggest chokers in baseball history. Led by All-Star outfielder Johnny Callison, third baseman and National League Rookie of Year Dick Allen, and pitching ace Jim Bunning, the Phillies, with a 90–60 record, held a six-and-a-half game lead over the rest of the league with two weeks to go in the season. It looked like Philadelphia was a lock, and the Phillies began printing World Series tickets. The team then lost an amazing and agonizing 10 games in a row to throw the pennant race into a wide-open three-team affair between the Phillies, the St. Louis Cardinals, and the Cincinnati Reds.

On the next-to-last day of the season, the Reds and Cardinals were tied for first with records of 92–69. The Phillies were one game back at 91–70. When October 4, 1964, dawned, the three contenders found themselves staring at a three-way tie if the

Phillies beat the Reds and the Cardinals lost to the New York Mets. As it happened, the Phillies did beat the Reds at Crosley Field, but the Cardinals whipped the Mets 11–5 to win the pennant, one game ahead of both the Reds and Phillies, who finished tied for second with 92–70 records. The Phillies have been excoriated ever since, and it is their big-time collapse that has kept the Reds substantial collapse of their own pretty much hidden in the shadows.

During Philadelphia's 10-game losing streak, the Reds pulled off a three-game sweep at Connie Mack Stadium, September 21, 22, and 23, which was highlighted by John Tsitouris's 1–0 complete game shutout. After they took a doubleheader from the Mets at Shea Stadium on September 27, the Reds ran their winning streak to nine games. They held a one-game lead over Philadelphia and a one-and-a-half-game lead over St. Louis with five games to play, all in Cincinnati at Crosley Field. The Reds lost four of those five games and kissed the 1964 pennant good-bye.

The Reds lost 2–0 to Pittsburgh on September 29. The next night they lost 1–0 in 16 innings on a suicide squeeze. They stranded 18 base runners in the game, 13 of them from the ninth through the fourteenth innings. They kept their pennant hopes alive by salvaging the final game of the Pittsburgh series, 5–4, on October 1. At the end of that day they trailed the first-place Cards by one game. The Reds had two games left with the Phillies, while the Cardinals had three to play with the Mets. The Reds' fate was pretty much decided by their next game, on October 2.

The Reds led 3–0 when the Phillies' Chris Short drilled Reds shortstop Leo Cardenas in the back with a pitch in the bottom of the seventh inning. Cardenas felt that the pitch was intentional, and he headed toward the mound waving his bat menacingly. Phillies catcher Clay Dalrymple headed Cardenas off, and other Reds players pulled him back toward first base. In the top of the eighth Cardenas was apparently still sulking over having gotten plunked, and he allowed a very catchable pop fly off the bat of Frank Thomas to fall in for a hit. That opened the floodgates, and the suddenly awakened Phillies scored four times in the inning to take a 4–3 lead, which is how the game ended. That same night the Mets beat the Cardinals (ending St. Louis's eight-game winning streak), which meant that the Reds' loss cost them a chance to take a half-game lead over St. Louis. The Reds were furious with Cardenas for having woken up the Phillies, especially starting pitcher Jim O'Toole, who had been sailing along before Cardenas let Thomas's pop-up drop in. O'Toole threw Cardenas up against a wall in the Reds clubhouse, and after teammates pulled O'Toole away from the suddenly very unpopular shortstop, Cardenas came after O'Toole with a screwdriver.

Did the tough loss to the Phillies and the clubhouse confrontation between O'Toole and Cardenas wake up the Reds and bring out their fighting spirit? Hardly. They went down meekly to the Phillies in the season's final game the next day 10–0, and that was that. Reds fans have often wondered how the Reds could win the 1961 pennant and then not win again until 1970. It wasn't that Reds teams during those years were devoid of talent; in fact, the 1964 Reds had plenty of it. Their offense was led by Frank Robinson, Vada Pinson, Pete Rose, and Deron Johnson, and they had the top pitching staff in the National League. The 1964 pennant was theirs for the taking. They didn't win it because they choked.

# NUMBERS DON'T LIE (OR DO THEY?)

f you don't realize that statistics ("the numbers" as they are commonly called) are extremely important in baseball, well, you just haven't been paying close attention. In the old days, stats were primitive and people assumed they meant exactly what they appeared to mean. If one guy batted .310, it was obvious he was a better hitter than a guy who batted. 275. That was good enough for people inside the game, when they paid any attention to stats at all. Many times they preferred, as they often put it, "to trust their eyes," which meant that for player evaluations they simply went by the impressions they formed by watching players play. Hardly scientific and increasingly unsatisfactory to fans who wanted better and more reliable information that would lead to real knowledge about players' abilities and usefulness. The statistical knowledge movement started slowly, around the 1950s; gathered steam with the founding of SABR (the Society for American Baseball Research) in the early 1970s; and turned into a bona fide revolution in the 1980s and 1990s, by which time just about all major league teams had become more cognizant of the potential value of certain types of statistical analysis. Completely new stats were invented—as well as new methods of studying some of the more traditional ones—and an avalanche of information about every player became widely available. We did get some pretty good answers to some age-old baseball questions, such as "Does it pay to bring the infield in to cut off a run early in the game?" But oddly, other questions, especially arguments about the relative merits of comparable players, have become more complicated and confusing than ever. The answer to the question "Can statistics tell us what we want to know?" is definitely "It depends." In other words, baseball stats are like bikinis: they show a lot, but not everything. Let's examine some aspects of Reds history that may, or may not, be clarified by a closer look at the pertinent numbers.

# IS DAVE CONCEPCION A HALL OF FAMER?

The sportswriters who vote in elections for the National Baseball Hall of Fame in Cooperstown (those who have covered major league baseball for at least 10 years as a member of the Baseball Writers Association of America) have decided that former Reds shortstop Dave Concepcion is not a Hall of Famer. In his first year (1994) on the Hall of Fame ballot, Concepcion received 31 votes for 6.8 percent of the vote, barely enough to remain on the ballot (5 percent is the minimum support required to stay on the ballot for another year, and to be elected a player must appear on 75 percent of the total votes in any particular year).

Concepcion received 43 votes the next year for a percentage of 9.3, and his support peaked in 1998 with 80 votes for a 16.9 percent total, far below the 75 percent threshold needed for election. In 2007, when Cal Ripken Jr. and Tony Gwynn were selected as first-ballot inductees, Concepcion appeared on the ballot for the 14th time, his next-to-last chance to be elected by the writers because 15 years is the maximum stay on the ballot annually considered by the sportswriters. Concepcion's 13.6 percent score in his 14th try implies that the writers are not going to elect him to the Hall of Fame.

Of course, after he falls off the writers' ballot, Concepcion will be eligible to be selected by the Veterans Committee, a sort of appeals panel that reviews and corrects or supplements the work done by the writers. But no matter who is doing the voting, the question remains, is Dave Concepcion a Hall of Famer?

To answer this question we must first begin with Concepcion's record, which the writers have concluded is a good one, just not good enough. David played 19 years in the major leagues and all of those years with one team, the Cincinnati Reds. This fact apparently has not impressed the writers, but it is a meaningful indication of a player's value, as no team keeps a player around that long who is not making a significant contribution. If stability means nothing, then why were Ripken's and Gwynn's one-team careers repeatedly referred to and praised during the coverage of their induction in 2007? It is at least interesting to note that all players who spent their entire careers of the same length as Concepcion's (19 years or more) with the same team are in the Hall of Fame, except for Mel Harder, Alan Trammell, Lou Whitaker, and Barry Larkin.

Concepcion batted .267 and finished with 2,326 hits. He won five Gold Glove Awards (1974, 1975, 1976, 1977, and 1979), and two Louisville Silver Slugger Awards (for best hitter at his position, 1981 and 1982). He was named to nine National League All-Star teams and two *Sporting News* major league All-Star teams, and he won the MVP Award in the 1982 All-Star Game. He also played in five League Championship Series and four World Series, batting .351 in 14 playoff games and .266 in 20 World Series contests for a total of 30 postseason hits.

Since the demands of each position on the baseball field are different, it has become standard procedure to compare a candidate not to all Hall of Famers but to those who played the same position as the candidate. Concepcion's record does not compare favorably to that of Honus Wagner, but Wagner was the Babe Ruth of shortstops. He is far above other shortstops in the Hall. Concepcion's record also falls considerably short of that of Cal Ripken Jr., but that is not a disqualifier either—although it is more of a problem for Davey, which we will get into later—as Ripken immediately upon his induction vaulted to the head of the class with Robin Yount as the shortstops first in line behind Wagner. The point here is that while Concepcion was no Wagner or Ripken, his record does stand up nicely when compared to many of the other shortstops certified as the greatest in history.

# RIBBIES FOR DAVEY

When Tony Perez backers were marshalling support for his election to the National Baseball Hall of Fame, they kept hammering away at Doggie's career RBI total as the key to persuading voters that he was qualified to join baseball's elite in Cooperstown. Supporters of Dave Concepcion for the same honor should do likewise. Concepcion is regarded as a Hall of Fame–quality fielder, so the holdup must be his image as an offensive player. Runs batted in is a highly regarded batting statistic, and here Concepcion comes off quite well in comparison to the other shortstops in the Hall of Fame. David's 950 RBIs rank him above all of the following Hall of Fame shortstops: Luis Aparicio, Arky Vaughan, Travis Jackson, Hughie Jennings, John Ward, Ozzie Smith, Bobby Wallace, Dave Bancroft, Lou Boudreau, Joe Tinker, Rabbit Maranville, Pee Wee Reese, and Phil Rizzuto. As the following list shows, only eight shortstops have driven in more runs in their careers than Concepcion.

1. Honus Wagner 1,732
2. Cal Ripken Jr. 1,695
3. Ernie Banks 1,636
4. George Davis 1,437
5. Joe Cronin 1,424
6. Robin Yount 1,406
7. Luke Appling 1,116
8. Joe Sewell 1,055
9. Dave Concepcion 950

So what is it that keeps the writers from voting for Concepcion? At least three things, the first of which is an anti–Big Red Machine bias. Although I can't prove it, I believe the writers have decided that, with Johnny Bench, Joe Morgan, and Tony Perez (not to mention manager Sparky Anderson), there are enough players from the Big Red Machine in the Hall of Fame already. Three may not sound like too many to you, but keep in mind that Pete Rose is in a real sense the fourth Big Red Machine

Hall of Famer. Everyone knows that he is being kept out of the Hall on a technicality. As unlikely as it looks at the present time that Rose will ever get into the Hall of Fame without buying a ticket—if he would be allowed in even then—there is always the possibility that he may be reinstated and selected. And as I say, in everyone's mind Rose *is* a Hall of Fame player. He just doesn't have the plaque.

And what's wrong with recognizing that the Big Red Machine had five Hall of Fame worthy players, anyway? The Brooklyn Dodgers, that's what. New York City is the media capitol of the world and of baseball, and there is a strong New York bias in Hall of Fame voting, not all of it coming from writers who live in the New York area or who cover New York teams. Thanks to Roger Kahn and to lionizers of Jackie Robinson, the Brooklyn Dodgers of the 1950s have attained a legendary, almost sacred status; that should not be undercut, the thinking goes, by a team from the unsophisticated Midwest, which was led by an ignorant bully and gambling crook like Pete Rose and an arrogant egomaniac like Johnny Bench (who actually thinks he was better than Roy Campanella, not to mention Yogi Berra and Thurman Munson!). Since the Brooklyn Dodgers only have four Hall of Famers, the Reds should only have four Hall of Famers.

This comparison between the Reds and Dodgers is not an idle one, and in fact the teams, from a Hall of Fame perspective, are remarkably alike. Both teams have their catchers and second basemen in the Hall of Fame, and both second basemen were heady players whose base-running abilities were a very disruptive weapon. The Dodgers' Pee Wee Reese teamed up with Robinson as best friends and double-play partners, and Rose, while not a short-stop like Reese, teamed with Morgan in every other meaningful way: as friends, as locker mates, and as a one-two or one-three punch at the top of the batting order. The Dodgers' Duke Snider (center field) and the Reds' Tony Perez (third and first base) did not play the same position, but both were counted on by their teams to hit home runs and to drive in runs. Furthermore, both teams went through agonizing defeats before finally getting over the hump and winning a world championship, and both teams had very good, but not so great, pitching. There is one more connection between the two teams—namely, a fifth player who keeps knocking on the door of the Hall of Fame but can't seem to gain entrance: Concepcion for the Reds, of course, and first baseman Gil Hodges for the Dodgers.

The most interesting thing of all is that it makes the most sense to compare Concepcion and Hodges not with each other, but Concepcion with his Dodgers counterpart, Pee Wee Reese, and Hodges with his Reds counterpart, Tony Perez. Let's take a look at their numbers.

Perez played 23 years in the big leagues, Hodges 18. Consequently, it's no surprise that Perez had more hits (2,732 to Hodges' 1,921) and more RBIs (1,652 to 1,274). Both of these advantages for Perez are a direct result of Tony's having a longer career and not necessarily of his being a better player, and while Perez rode his supposedly exceptional talent for racking up RBIs into the Hall, in fact Hodges had the same number of 100+ RBI seasons that Perez did: seven. Hodges batted .273 for his career; Perez, .279; virtually no difference there. The same with home runs: 379 for Perez, 370 for Hodges. Tony did bang out 505 doubles to only 295 for Hodges, but Perez had 2,748 more at-bats to get those extra doubles in. On the other side of the coin, in those extra at-bats Perez struck out 730 more times than Hodges did, while drawing 18 fewer bases on balls. It is also not surprising, therefore, that it is Hodges who came out with the better on-base percentage (.359 to .341) and the better slugging percentage (.487 to .463). If anybody can take these numbers and prove that Perez was a substantially better player than Hodges, that person should be put in charge of reducing the national debt. That said, I'm not saying that Tony Perez does not belong in the Hall of Fame—I think he does. However, based on the numbers, if Perez is in, then Hodges probably should be in, too.

That brings us back to Dave Concepcion and Pee Wee Reese. Based on their numbers, if Reese is in, Concepcion should be, too. Concepcion played three years longer than Reese and has cumulative advantages in hits (2,326 to 2,170), doubles (389 to 330), RBIs (950 to 885), and stolen bases (321 to 232). However, in

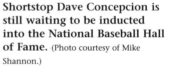

DAVID CONCEPCION #13
NUMBER RETIREMENT – AUGUST 25, 2007

Shortstop Dave Concepcion is still waiting to be inducted into the National Baseball Hall of Fame. (Photo courtesy of Mike Shannon.)

almost 700 fewer at-bats Reese hit more home runs (126 to 101) and had more walks (1,210 to 736) and fewer strikeouts (890 to 1,186). While the two players had almost identical batting averages (Reese .269; Concepcion .267), Reese finished his career with a better on-base percentage (.366 to .322) and a higher slugging percentage (.377 to .357). Amazingly, Concepcion compares with Reese in almost the same exact ways that Perez compares with Hodges. The two Reds players played longer and so have advantages in some of the glamorous cumulative statistical categories; the two Dodgers have advantages in more unsung statistical categories and in batting percentages, which suggest that they were better overall offensive performers than their Reds counterparts. Nevertheless, the two pairs of players are so close in their numbers that, again, if one of them is Hall of Fame worthy then the other one probably is, too. What this means, given the anti–Big Red Machine bias that exists, is that Dave Concepcion is not going to be admitted to the Hall of Fame unless and until Gil Hodges is admitted.

Unfortunately, there are two more barriers, of recent erection, blocking Concepcion's path to the Hall of Fame. The first one is the redefinition of the shortstop position, brought about by the likes of Ripken and Alex Rodriguez, and to a lesser extent Yount, Derek Jeter, and Barry Larkin. These players have hit the long ball at rates far greater than average shortstops of the past, and so the expectations for the position have changed. Shortstop is still not considered a power position to the same degree as the corners are, but ballclubs today definitely want more homers out of the position than in the past. More to the point as far as Concepcion is concerned, many Hall of Fame voters undoubtedly are holding him to a home run standard that did not exist when he played.

The second additional barrier in Concepcion's way is Barry Larkin himself. Larkin is considered a future Hall of Famer— perhaps not a first-ballot Hall of Famer, but a pretty sure bet to eventually make it. Larkin immediately succeeded Concepcion at short for the Reds, and many voters, already penciling in Larkin sometime in a future election, are probably reluctant now to vote for Concepcion, reasoning that the Reds couldn't have fielded two Hall of Fame shortstops in a row.

Since Dave Concepcion will not be elected to the Hall of Fame by sportswriters, should he be selected by the Veterans Committee? Yes, he should, and the reasoning behind that answer is simple: the best players at their positions in each league each decade or so should be in the Hall of Fame. And Dave Concepcion was the best shortstop in the National League for a significant period of time for which the Hall of Fame has no representative at his position from either league.

The logic behind this contention is inescapable. The major leagues at all times, by definition, are manned by the best baseball players available. For example, whoever the starting shortstops were on the eight teams that played in the National League in 1936 were eight of the best shortstops on the planet at that time (the world's other eight best shortstops were playing in the American League). Now, whoever was the best of the best of that

# TOP 10 REDS NUMBER-ONE DRAFT CHOICES

The June free agent draft of amateur players began in 1965, and few things are as important to the success of a baseball franchise as doing well in this selection competition. Every major league organization invests a lot of time, work, and money into the process, and mistakes are very costly. Ideally, a number-one draft choice will become a star like Alex Rodriguez or Ken Griffey Jr. He should at least make the major leagues, and if he doesn't, he is considered a flop. The Reds have drafted fairly well over the years, but hardly flawlessly. Four of the team's first five draft choices—Bernie Carbo, Gary Nolan, Wayne Simpson, and Don Gullett—turned out to be fine players. Seven of the next eight never made it to the majors: shortstop Gary Polcynski, pitcher Larry Payne, outfielder Brad Kessler, pitcher Steve Reed, outfielder Tony Moretto, pitcher Mark King, and third baseman Tad Vegner. The 1978 pick, Nick Esasky, ended the string of bad picks. Here are the

**Drafting shortstop Barry Larkin in 1985 would prove to be the best selection in the team's history.** (Photo courtesy of Getty Images.)

10 best number-one draft picks made by the Reds based on career with the Reds (June amateur draft; overall pick in parentheses):

1. Barry Larkin 1985 (4)
2. Gary Nolan 1966 (13)
3. Don Gullett 1969 (14)
4. Austin Kearns 1998 (7)
5. Nick Esasky 1978 (17)
6. Pokey Reese 1991 (20)
7. Wayne Simpson 1967 (8)
8. Ron Robinson 1980 (19)
9. Brett Tomko 1995 (54, 2nd rd.)
10. Bernie Carbo 1965 (16)

group of 16 players deserves to be included in Cooperstown no matter how he stacks up, or appears to stack up from our vantage point, to the shortstops of other periods. And it might easily be the case that two or three shortstops who were active that year deserve to be in the Hall. As it so happens, there were two shortstops, one in each league, playing that year who became Hall of Famers: Arky Vaughan of the Pittsburgh Pirates and Luke Appling of the Chicago White Sox. Vaughan batted .335 that year, good for fifth in the NL; Appling batted .388 to lead the AL.

Today there are 21 shortstops (not counting Negro Leaguers) in the Hall of Fame. If we divide baseball history into decades and then also into 20-year periods, and place these shortstops into the decades and 20-year spans that correspond (as closely as possible) to the careers of the players, most decades and every 20-year period are represented by at least one Hall of Fame shortstop. For instance, the 1920–1930 decade is represented by the Indians' and Yankees' Joe Sewell, whose relatively brief career ran between 1920 and 1933. The 1920–1940 period is represented by National Leaguer Travis Jackson of the New York Giants (1922–1936) and by American Leaguer Joe Cronin, who spent all but a smidgen of his career with the Washington Senators and the Boston Red Sox (1926–1945). The only 20-year period without a Hall of Fame shortstop, from either league, is 1960–1980. Now, Concepcion's career (1970–1988) fits nicely into the 1970–1990 20-year slot, and one shortstop from the period is in the Hall of Fame, Robin Yount. But Yount only takes care of the American League. It makes sense to argue that the best shortstop in the National League during that time deserves to join Yount. Since there is that gaping hole in the 1960–1980 period, and since Concepcion was the National League's best shortstop for most of the 1970s, he is the man. (Concepcion's selection would still not take care of the 1960–1970 decade, but there are at least two other shortstops worth serious consideration who would take care of it: Dick Groat and Maury Wills, who each won an NL MVP Award among their other accomplishments.)

If you have any doubt that Concepcion really was the best shortstop of the 1970s, in either league, remember that he was named to nine National League All-Star teams, seven of which took place between 1970 and 1980. During that period Bert Campaneris led AL shortstops in All-Star Game selections with five; Freddie Patek, Rick Burleson, and Toby Harrah tied for second with three selections each. As for the NL, Davey's main competition came from Larry Bowa of the Philadelphia Phillies, who was selected to five All-Star Games, followed by Don Kessinger with four, and Chris Speier and Bill Russell, who made it onto three All-Star Game rosters each. Bowa and Concepcion enjoyed a friendly rivalry, and their careers were similar. While Bowa led the NL in fielding percentage six times to Concepcion's once, fielding percentage can be the most misleading of all statistics—a fielder with no range may make fewer errors, but he probably helps his team less than a player with more range and more errors—and there is little evidence that Bowa was a better overall fielder than the slick, reliable Concepcion. In fact, according to a statistic called Fielding Runs, which measures how many runs a player saves or costs his team, Concepcion had the better glove by far. And don't forget Concepcion's five Gold Gloves, compared to the single Gold Glove won by Bowa.

So what does all this mean in the end? Nothing if enough members of the Veterans Committee don't take the time to fairly consider Concepcion's qualifications and also to realize that his selection would be the only reasonable choice to fill that gaping hole in the decade-by-decade representation of shortstops in the Hall of Fame. Davey will make it one day, Reds fans, but it won't be easy, and his selection, as I said earlier, will probably come only after that of Gil Hodges, which I think will also happen. What Davey needs is a campaign, an orchestrated attempt to gently pressure the powers-that-be into making the right choice. Such a thing has been done before, believe me.

# REDS HOME-RUN KING (NOT WHO YOU THINK)

George Foster hit 52 home runs in 1977 to set the Reds record for home runs in a single season. Foster broke the old Reds record of 49, which had been set in 1954 by first baseman Ted Kluszewski. While terrorizing National League pitchers that season, Foster used a black bat that was as uncommon for the time as the number of homers he blasted. Back then, in baseball's pre-steroid period, a 50-home-run season was an eye-popping accomplishment that marked a hitter as one of the game's all-time great sluggers. Before Foster blasted 52 homers in 1977, only eight other players in baseball history had ever reached the 50-in-a-season mark, and those eight players had done it a total of 15 times. (Jimmie Foxx, Ralph Kiner, Willie Mays, and Mickey Mantle had done it twice, while the Babe swatted 50 or more in a season four different times.) The difficulty of the feat in the pre-steroid era is further evidenced by the fact that nobody reached the magic 50 pinnacle again until 1990, when the massive Cecil Fielder knocked 50 balls out of the park for the Detroit Tigers. Things began to change in the middle of that decade. Albert Belle hit 50 home runs for the Cleveland Indians in 1995, and from that point until the end of the 2007 season, the 50-home-run mark has been reached or surpassed another 22 times; Alex Rodriguez (54) and Prince Fielder (50) did it most recently, in 2007.

Foster's 52 home runs in 1977 remain the most ever hit in one season by a Reds player, and his record, a true one untainted by the dishonest use of performance-enhancing drugs, should be celebrated and appreciated. In a real sense, however, Foster is not the

**The mercurial Kevin Mitchell was one of the most efficient home-run hitters in Reds history.** (Photo courtesy of Getty Images.)

single-season home-run king of the Cincinnati Reds. Who is? Well, let me explain.

Let's say you follow a basketball team that has two guards who do almost all their shooting from the outside (but not from behind the three-point line). One of these guards averages five baskets on 10 shots a game, while the second guard averages 10 baskets a game on 30 shots. The second guard averages 20 points a game, the first guard only 10 points, but nobody would call the second guard the better shooter. What we are talking about is shooting percentage, which is just as important, if not more important, than the number of points scored. The same thing applies to home-run hitting, just as it does to hitting overall, despite the fact that fans seldom consider a player's home-run percentage, which is the number of home runs a player hits every 100 at-bats. Home-run percentage can be calculated for a player's season or for his entire career, and it is a way to compare players' efficiency in hitting home runs (to calculate home-run percentage, you divide the homers by the at-bats).

So what was Foster's home-run percentage in 1977? Based on his 52 homers in 615 at-bats, Foster's home-run percentage was a league-leading 8.5 percent, which means that George hit an average of eight and a half homers every 100 times he came to bat. Pretty good, but not the best in Reds history. In 1954, when Ted Kluszewski hit 49 home runs in 573 at-bats, his home-run percentage was a slightly better 8.6 percent. Big Klu's rate was also good enough to lead the league, and it led all Reds sluggers for many years, until a squat slugger built like a powder keg—with a temperament to match—broke Klu's mark in 1994.

Outfielder Kevin Mitchell came to Cincinnati in November of 1992 in a trade that sent Reds pitcher Norm Charlton to the Seattle Mariners. Injuries, weight problems, and his inability to stay out of trouble kept Mitchell from realizing his enormous potential. As a former gang member who had been shot more than once, Mitchell was fortunate to have made it to the majors at all. His peak year in the majors (1989) with the San Francisco Giants showed what he was capable of doing. That year he won the NL MVP Award for hitting .291 while leading the National League in home runs (47) and RBIs (125). He almost garnered more notoriety for one fielding play that year than for his lusty batting when, overrunning a fly ball in the left-field corner, he reached up and caught the ball bare-handed. By the time the Reds acquired Mitchell, his career was in decline. Still, in 1994 he produced as never before. In only 310 at-bats, Mitchell hit 30 home runs, good for a home-run percentage of 9.7, the best in Reds history. Mitchell got so few at-bats because the players went on strike on August 12, canceling the rest of the 1994 season. Had Mitchell been able to bat 600 times in 1994 and continue hitting home runs at the same pace, he would have finished the season with 58 home runs. As it was, Mitchell also set a new Reds record for slugging percentage—his .681 eclipsed the old mark of .642 set by Kluszewski in 1954. Mitchell's slugging percentage was so high because almost half (49 of 101) of his hits that year went for extra bases. George Foster will never be dislodged from his place of honor until somebody in a Reds uniform hits more than 52 home runs in one season. But the chubby masher with the gold front teeth who hit home runs at a faster pace (for half a season) than any other player in team history, Kevin "World" Mitchell, should not be forgotten either.

# THE SHORT, BITTER LIFE (AS A MANAGER) OF TONY PEREZ

Everybody in baseball knows that managers are hired to be fired. Tony Perez knew that too when the Reds hired him to be the club's 42nd manager on October 30, 1992. Tony just never dreamed that he'd be fired only 44 games into the 1993 season, making his tenure the shortest in Reds history for any manager who started the season at the helm (and did not take over at some point after the season had started).

Nobody doubted that Tony Perez was a highly qualified baseball man. Many people thought he would one day be elected to the Baseball Hall of Fame (as he was in 2000), and he had served on the Reds coaching staff since 1986. Reds fans were upset with the resignation (on October 6, 1992) of Lou Piniella, who decided he'd had enough of owner Marge Schott's interference, and the hiring of Perez was seen by some as an attempt to calm the waters. Other observers saw the hiring of Perez as a calculated attempt by Schott—who had come under increasing fire for her attitudes towards minorities—to curry favor with the power structure in Major League Baseball and with the media, which had been very critical of those same attitudes. Perez was probably naïve to believe that the Reds simply felt that he was the best man available for the job, but he did believe that.

In 1993 the Reds got off to the team's worst start (2–9) since 1955, which was hardly helped by a spring training injury that sidelined the regular first baseman, Hal Morris, until June. Over the next 26 games, though, the team turned things around, going 17–9, and left town for a West Coast road trip riding a seven-game winning streak. The Reds lost six of seven in Los Angeles and San Francisco and came home with a 20–24 record. The next morning (May 24), general manager Jim Bowden woke Perez with a phone call. "I've got bad news for you," Bowden said.

"What is it?" said the half-awake Perez, thinking that something had happened to one of his players.

"We just fired you," said Bowden, who had to repeat himself before his message sank in.

Perez was angry and perplexed at being given such a short trial period and insulted that Bowden had fired him over the phone instead of face to face. The fans were angry, too, at seeing one of their all-time favorites treated so cavalierly, and during the game the next day against Atlanta five airplanes, trailing messages protesting Tony's dismissal, flew over Riverfront Stadium.

Perez landed on his feet, hired a month later by the Florida Marlins as director of international relations and special assistant to the general manager. He also did some on-field coaching for the Marlins and became their manager in 2001 when the Marlins fired John Boles 48 games into the season. Boles was fired after being publicly criticized by Marlins pitcher Dan Miceli, who said 90 percent of the players on the team thought Boles made stupid moves during the games and didn't respect him because he had never played in the major leagues. At first, Perez took the job reluctantly and only temporarily, citing outside business interests that would conflict with the demands of the managerial job. After a week at the helm, he said that he thought the Marlins did respect his leadership, and so he managed the team through the end of the season. Under Perez the Marlins played slightly better baseball (54–60) for a .474 winning percentage (compared to .458 under Boles), but the team actually dropped from third (where they were when Boles was fired) to fourth at season's end. When the year ended, Tony showed he'd had enough of managing by returning, at his own request, to his job in the front office.

So how good a manager was Tony Perez? Well, there really isn't that much evidence to go on. The Cincinnati media criticized him for his game management and for the mental mistakes

# PETE ROSE'S MILESTONE HITS

Pete Rose's march toward becoming baseball's all-time hit king seems like an inevitability today. In reality, it was no such thing. To pull off the feat required not only Rose's monomaniacal drive, but also luck, in terms of his being able to avoid any serious injury, and the near perfect circumstances of his being able to continually wind up where he was able to stay in the lineup, despite his decreasing productivity. This in no way is meant to belittle his great achievement, which seems today to be unassailable by others. The easiest way to grasp how difficult it would be to break Rose's record for career hits is to consider the following statement: if you got 200 hits a year for 20 years, you would still be behind the hit king. Here are Rose's milestone hits on his way to batting immortality.

| No. | Date | Type | Pitcher | Opponent |
|-----|------|------|---------|----------|
| 1 | 4–13–63 | Triple | Bob Friend | Pittsburgh |
| 500 | 9–16–65 | Single | Al Jackson | at New York |
| 1,000 | 6–26–68 | Single | Dick Selma | New York |
| 1,500 | 8–29–70 | Single | Carl Morton | at Montreal |
| 2,000 | 6–19–73 | Single | Ron Bryant | at San Francisco |
| 2,500 | 8–17–75 | Single | Bruce Kison | Pittsburgh |
| 3,000 | 5–5–78 | Single | Steve Rogers | Montreal |
| 3,500 | 8–15–80 | Single | Tom Hausman | at New York |
| 3,631* | 8–10–81 | Single | Mark Littell | St. Louis |
| 3,772# | 6–22–82 | Double | John Stuper | at St. Louis |
| 4,000+ | 4–13–84 | Double | Jerry Koosman | Philadelphia |
| 4,192** | 9–11–85 | Single | Eric Show | San Diego |
| 4,256## | 8–14–86 | Single | Greg Minton | San Francisco |

* Set all-time NL record for hits; was playing for Phillies

# Moved past Hank Aaron and into second place all-time

+ Became first player in NL history to reach 4,000 hits

** Passed Ty Cobb to claim hits-leader title

## Rose's last hit; his career total of 4,256 may never be equaled

the team made, and Bowden apparently thought that he wasn't motivating the team sufficiently. Perez was most likely never Jim Bowden's man in the first place—Bowden pressured Perez into signing a one-year take-it-or-leave-it contract and refused to let him assemble his own hand-picked coaching staff. In fact, there were major managerial replacement candidates all over the place, still in the Reds employment. Davey Johnson took over the Reds when Perez was fired, and though a slew of additional injuries (which occurred after Perez was fired) completely derailed the team for 1993, Johnson led the Reds to a first-place finish in the strike-shortened season of 1994 and a Central Division championship in 1995. This significant improvement, coupled with the second-place finish (and 90–72 record) of the team under Piniella the year before Perez was hired, does not cast Perez's record as Reds manager in a particularly flattering light. On the other hand, 44 games was simply not a fair test of the man's ability to manage a major league ballclub.

You particularly smart Reds fans are probably saying to yourselves right now that the Reds didn't have a winning record when Tony got the axe, but a lot depends on how good a team a manager has to work with. No argument about that here. In fact, there is a pretty good way to measure how well a manager does with the material he gets to work with, and I don't mean his winning percentage, which merely states how well the team did, not how well it *should* have done.

Managerial projected wins is a stat that tells us how many games a team won compared to the number of games it was projected to win based on its run production (i.e., the difference between the number of runs the team scored and the number of runs it allowed). A positive number is good; a negative number is bad. Even though his sample is very small, Perez's projected wins with the Reds was -0.3, which means that the team won just about exactly the number of games it should have won. With the Marlins, Perez's number dropped to -2.9, which means that the Marlins underperformed for Tony by about 3 games. In his three-plus seasons as Marlins manager, John Boles led Florida to almost five (+4.8) more wins than they were projected to get.

Projected wins also gives us some better insight into how other Reds managers did, beyond what winning percentage tells us. Sparky Anderson is the leader among Reds managers in total wins and winning percentage. He is in the Hall of Fame and he won championships in both leagues, yet some people claim he was merely a push-button manager with great players. They should stop claiming that—Sparky has the highest projected wins of any Reds manager with +32.3. According to the stat, he turned in his best jobs in 1970 (+11.6 wins) and, ironically, in 1978 (+9.3), the off year that led to his firing by Dick Wagner. Sparky's projected wins for 1975 and 1976 were +1.3 and -1.2.

Second among the Reds managers who are in the top 10 according to winning percentage is John McNamara. Mac has not been considered by public opinion to have been a particularly good manager, but during his Reds career he managed his teams to 19 more wins than they were projected to earn. Third on the list is Bill McKechnie with +18 projected wins, including +2.5 and +4.5 during the two years (1939 and 1940) when the Reds won National League pennants. Fred Hutchinson comes in fourth at +16.9, including a score of +10.3 in the pennant-winning year of 1961; Dave Bristol rounds out the top five with +7.7.

The remainder of the top 10 includes Pat Moran, +6.9 (including +6.0 for the 1919 season); Jack McKeon, +.8; and three managers who had negative scores for their careers as Reds skippers: Dick Sisler, -1.7; Davey Johnson, -3.1; and Joe Kelley, -10.3.

There are three men who rank among the Reds' 10 most winningest managers but who do not hold one of the top 10 winning percentages: Jack Hendricks, Birdie Tebbetts, and Pete Rose. Hendricks won 469 games and lost 450, and according to his projected win total of -.2 his teams did just about what they were supposed to do. Tebbetts won 372 games and lost 357, but he apparently had more talent to work with than Hendricks, as his more negative score (-10.6) indicates.

And what about Pete Rose, a man, like John McNamara, not highly regarded in most circles as a great Reds manager? Pete's Reds teams won 17.7 more games than they should have according to their run production, a performance that places Pete fourth among all Reds skippers. Apparently, Rose knew what he was doing in the dugout.

## ACE OF THE REDS BULLPEN

Relief pitching is more important in baseball today than ever before, and the roles of the members in the bullpen have become more and more specialized. Earned-run average is still an important measure of effectiveness for relievers, just as it is for starting pitchers, but the save has become the coin of the realm for relief pitchers. As far as the average fan is concerned, the more saves a relief pitcher has, the better a pitcher he is. Going into the 2007 season, the top five career leaders in saves for the Cincinnati Reds were Danny Graves (182), John Franco (148), Clay Carroll (119), and Jeff Brantley, Rob Dibble, and Tom Hume, all tied with 88.

Such a simple totaling of the number of saves a reliever earns leaves something to be desired in telling us how effective he really is. If reliever A gets twice as many opportunities to save a game as reliever B gets, then reliever A should have more saves than reliever B. But in obtaining more saves, perhaps reliever A also blows a lot more saves than reliever B, and isn't really doing a better job than reliever B. What we need to know then is the relationship between the number of saves a pitcher earns and the number of opportunities he was given in which to earn those saves. That relationship is called save percentage, and it may give us a different picture of who is really the ace of the Reds bullpen.

For a single season, a save percentage over 90 is outstanding, as going into the 2007 season slightly more than 50 seasons of a save percentage higher than 90 had been recorded. Believe it or not, two perfect seasons have been turned in: by Rod Beck, who saved 28 games in 28 tries in 1994, and by Eric Gagne, who saved 55 games in 55 opportunities in 2003. Gagne's perfect 2003 season for the Los Angeles Dodgers was part of his incredible streak of 84 saved games in a row without a blown save, a record that will not be broken anytime soon. Gagne's streak went from August 28, 2002, to July 5, 2004. Not surprisingly, Gagne also holds the career record for save percentage at an amazing 94.65.

According to the numbers, reliever Jeff Brantley is one of the best pitchers to ever grace the Cincinnati bullpen.

John Smoltz is second at 91.67, and third is Trevor Hoffman of the San Diego Padres at 89.26. Hoffman also boasts of having to his credit five seasons of save percentages of 92.7 or higher. It must pain Reds fans to hear about the great success of the stupendously consistent Hoffman, a definite future Hall of Famer who once belonged to Cincinnati. In fact, it was a Reds minor league manager, Jim Lett, who saved Hoffman's career at a crucial turning point. Hoffman started his pro career as a weak-hitting infielder, and when his time to prove himself had just about run out, Lett said, "Hey, Trevor, before we send you home for good, why don't we see if you can pitch?" Hoffman was an immediate sensation on the mound, striking out 52 in 33 innings and compiling a 1.87 ERA for Cedar Rapids, and the rest, as they say, is San Diego Padres history.

So how have Reds relievers fared in save percentage? Well, two Reds have turned in seasons good enough to make the top 50: Clay Carroll, who saved 37 out of 40 games in 1972 for 92.5 percent, and John Franco, who saved 39 out of 42 games in 1988 for 92.9 percent.

How a player does over the long haul is always more important than his short-term performance, so in order to identify the true ace of the Reds bullpen we have to look at the career save percentages of the guys who toiled in relief for Cincinnati for more than a season or two. Danny Graves always received a lot of criticism on Cincinnati sports talk radio stations for allowing a lot of blown saves. But did he really suffer an inordinate number of blown saves? The truth is, he didn't: his career save percentage with the Reds was 82.4 percent, good for the number-two spot on the list. John Franco (number two in saves) is third with 80.4 percent; Clay Carroll (number three in saves) is fourth with 76.8 percent; and Pedro Borbon (whose 76 saves do not put him in the top 5) moves into the fifth spot with a save percentage of 76. The best career save percentage for any Reds reliever belongs to one of the men tied for fifth place in saves, Jeff Brantley, who earned his 88 saves for the Reds in 105 opportunities. That gives the Cowboy an 83.8 save percentage and makes him the most reliable closer in Cincinnati Reds history.

## THE REDS ROOKIE OF THE YEAR YOU'VE NEVER HEARD OF

Seven Cincinnati Reds players have won the National League Rookie of the Year Award, which has also been known since 1988 as the Jackie Robinson Award. Frank Robinson was the first Red to win the award, in 1956, and he is the only Reds recipient to win the award unanimously. Robinson's sweep of the voting was well-deserved because he alone of Reds winners truly had a great year his rookie season. Frank batted .290 that year with 83 RBIs, and his 38 home runs tied him for second in the league behind Duke Snider's 43. In addition, the 38 home runs Robinson hit in 1956 set a National League record for rookies, which still stands today.

The other Reds winners of the Jackie Robinson Award are Pete Rose (1963), Tommy Helms (1966), Johnny Bench (1968), Pat Zachry (1976), Chris Sabo (1988), and Scott Williamson (1999). While not unanimous winners, all of these players won their Rookie of the Year Awards handily, except for Zachry, who tied San Diego Padres pitcher Butch Metzger and consequently shared the honor with him, and Bench, who edged out New York Mets pitcher Jerry Koosman (10.5 votes to 9.5 votes).

As good as Robinson's Rookie of the Year season was, it doesn't come close to the best rookie season ever turned in by a Reds player: the spectacular first-year performance of pitcher Billy Rhines. The only reason Rhines didn't win the National League Rookie of the Year Award is that he played before the award was inaugurated, in 1890. Had any such award been around, Rhines definitely would have taken it home. Not only did Billy win 28 games, he also led the league in earned-run average with a mark of 1.95. And those 28 wins are the most victories won in a single season by any Reds pitcher. The reason you always see the 27 wins by Dolf Luque (1923) and Bucky Walters (1939) cited as the Reds record is that the Reds themselves have established 1900 as the year when official records begin to be recognized.

A native of Ridgway, Pennsylvania, and an alumnus of Bucknell University, William Pearl "Billy" Rhines was a submarine-style pitcher who was playing for Davenport, Iowa, when soon-to-be Reds manager Tom Loftus spotted him. A native of Dubuque, Iowa, Loftus was named skipper of the Reds team that in 1890 rejoined the National League after a nine-year stint in the American Association. Loftus brought the 21-year-old Rhines and Billy's Davenport batterymate, Jeremiah Peter Harrington, with him to Cincinnati, and it was the best move he made all year.

Rhines was virtually unhittable in the first half of his rookie year, winning 18 of 20 decisions through July 7. He received less run support in the second half and may have tired a bit, too, as he pitched 401 innings on the year. In any event, he went 10–15 in the second half of the season to finish 28–17, but his ERA of 1.95 still led the league.

Rhines continued his workhorse ways the following year, pitching another 372 innings. He compiled a good ERA of 2.87 and won 17 games but somehow lost 24, perhaps because his mind was no longer completely on baseball. Rhines had discovered the night life, and in 1892 his drinking and carousing really began to affect his career. Two weeks before Opening Day, while trying to win a silly barroom bet that he could flip professional wrestler Walter Norman, Rhines broke his collar bone. Less than a month later he was suspended for two months after he and his buddy Harrington (along with a third Reds player) got into a brawl at a Cincinnati saloon. The injury and the suspension led to a poor season (4–7, 5.06 ERA) and an even more dismal record the following year with Louisville (1–4, 8.71). Rhines rebounded with two more good seasons for the Reds (winning 19 games in 1895 and 21 in 1897) before he finished out his baseball career with the Pittsburgh Pirates in 1898 and 1899. He returned to Ridgway, where he drove a taxi and hunted, earning a reputation as the best shot in the state, until his death from heart disease in 1922. He wound up being among the Reds' all-time leaders in wins, winning percentage, innings pitched, and complete games. He is unjustly forgotten by most fans, particularly in light of his club record 28 victories, but he did receive some belated recognition when STATS, Inc. named him the Ex Post Facto National League Rookie of the Year for 1890.

## REDS RETIRED NUMBERS

The greatest honor a major league baseball team can bestow on a player is that of retiring his uniform number. The first player to have his uniform number retired was Lou Gehrig, whose No. 4 was retired by the New York Yankees on July 4, 1939. Two other players, Carl Hubbell and Babe Ruth, had their numbers retired in the 1940s. After that, the practice fell into disuse for a long while. Number retirements have become much more common in the past two decades, but some of the more recently formed teams, such as the Seattle Mariners and the Arizona Diamondbacks, have still not retired any numbers. Naturally, almost invariably star players have been accorded this signal honor. The exceptions to the rule include Houston Astros pitcher Jim Umbricht (No. 32), whose number retirement was a way to remember his battle with cancer; managers; longtime coach Jimmie Reese (No. 50) of the California Angels; owners Gene Autry (No. 26) of the Angels and August Busch (No. 85) of the St. Louis Cardinals; and front office executive Carl Barger (No. 5) of the Florida Marlins. Some teams have even given the honor to players who never wore a number on their uniforms—the practice of using numbers on baseball uniforms did not catch on until 1929, when the Cleveland Indians wore numbers on their backs all season and eventually influenced other teams to follow suit. For instance, the Detroit Tigers include Ty Cobb among their players with retired numbers, even though Cobb played in the dead-ball era before numbers caught on.

The Cincinnati Reds have been fairly conservative in bestowing this greatest of all team honors, and the Reds first retired a number after the premature death of the highly respected and beloved manager Fred Hutchinson. Due to the enlightened influence of management, particularly that of CEO John Allen, the team has recently added enough members to this exclusive club to rank the Reds among the leaders of major league clubs with the most retired uniform numbers. In addition to the players and managers discussed below, two more Reds, at least, will one day have their numbers retired by the team: shortstop Barry Larkin and outfielder Ken Griffey Jr.

## No. 1 Fred Hutchinson (1965)

The first number to be retired by the Reds was the No. 1 worn by manager Frederick Charles Hutchinson. "Hutch," as he was called by everyone in baseball, had a 10-year career as a pitcher in the major leagues, all of it spent with the Detroit Tigers. The Tigers brokered a deal to acquire the tenacious young right-hander after he had fashioned a 25–7 record with a 2.48 ERA for Triple A Seattle in 1938 and earned the *Sporting News* Minor League Player of the Year Award. Although he never became the big winner the Tigers had hoped he would become, he did win in double figures six times (with a high of 18 wins in 1947) and finished with a 95–71 career record.

Despite being a pretty good pitcher, the thing Hutchinson became famous for was his terrible temper, which led to numerous incidents of wrecked furniture, punched-in walls, and overturned postgame meal spreads. Hutchinson didn't like losing any better as a manager than he had as a player, and if anything, his temper became worse and more legendary as a manager. His naturally dour facial expression and great physical strength added to his intimidating image, prompting Philadelphia sportswriter Larry Merchant to say, "Hutch doesn't throw furniture. He throws rooms"; and Reds first baseman Gordy Coleman to quip: "Man, if you put this guy in a cage with a bear, you'd have to bet on him, not the bear." Unbelievably, Hutchinson had a good rapport with his players, perhaps because they understood that he cared about them and that his anger was not directed at them. "I take it out on inanimate objects," he once explained. "I don't get mad at my friends or family." The players also respected him because, while he demanded excellence and the players' best efforts, he didn't criticize them in public.

Hutchinson started his managing career in the majors, in mid-season 1952. One day he was a member of the Tigers bullpen, and the next he was the team's manager, picked to succeed the dismissed Red Rolfe. He was fired after the 1954 season and returned to his hometown of Seattle, where he managed the Seattle Rainiers to the 1955 PCL pennant, which led to his second job in the majors, with the St. Louis Cardinals. The Cards' second-place finish in 1957 earned him a Manager of the Year Award, yet he was fired again after the 1958 season. When the Reds fired Mayo Smith with a 35–45 record on July 8, 1959, they named Hutchinson as his replacement.

The Reds improved under Hutch in '59 (39–35), took a step backwards in 1960 (67–87), but then surprised all of baseball by winning the franchise's first pennant in 21 years in 1961. Hutchinson was never fired by the Reds. A heavy smoker all his life, he began displaying the effects of lung cancer in 1963. In January of 1964 the ballclub made a public announcement confirming that Hutchinson had lung cancer. The Reds' skipper then underwent two months of radiation, which at the time was an experimental treatment. Hutch went through spring training with the ballclub and stayed at the helm once the season started. It was a struggle to get through each day, but Hutchinson stoically soldiered on. Everyone who witnessed his daily fight to live and to continue to lead his men marveled at his courage and lack of self-pity. "He showed us how to live, now he's showing us how to die," said Phillies manager Gene Mauch. On August 12 the Reds threw Hutch a 45th birthday party before the game at Crosley Field. The gaunt Hutchinson had lost a lot of weight, and after he spoke to the crowd, most parents had trouble explaining to their children why they were crying. The next day he resigned as manager of the team in order to rest and seek further treatments. He died on November 12 in Bradenton, Florida, and the Reds immediately retired his uniform number. He ranks fourth among Reds managers in total wins (446–375) and fifth in winning percentage (.543).

Hutch's brother, William B. Hutchinson, was one of the pioneers of research into cancer radiation treatments, and he and a host of Fred's friends raised the money to build the Fred Hutchinson Cancer Research Center in Seattle. A year after Hutchinson's death, the Fred Hutchinson Memorial Award was established to annually honor a major league player who "best exemplifies the character and fighting spirit of the late Fred Hutchinson" and "who overcomes any form of adversity." Mickey Mantle of the New York Yankees won the first award in 1965, and since then it has been given to six Cincinnati Reds players: Pete Rose (1968), Bobby Tolan (1972), Gary Nolan (1975), Johnny Bench (1981), Ron Oester (1988), and Sean Casey (1999). Ray Knight (1983) and Eric Davis (1997) also won the award, but not as Reds players.

## No. 5 Johnny Bench (August 11, 1984)

Johnny Bench was born in the small town of Binger, Oklahoma, and he was raised by his father from the very beginning to be a major league catcher. Bench focused on that goal, too, and as a youngster he practiced signing his name for the day his signature would be in demand. By the time he was a high school player, Bench's physical gifts and talents were so great and obvious that major league teams were aware of him despite the isolation of Binger. Nevertheless, Johnny was completely passed over in the first round of the June draft after his senior year in high school, as many teams attributed the glowing scouting reports on him to the inferior competition he had faced. Fortunately for the Reds, they selected him in the second round (after selecting Bernie Carbo in the first round).

It made little difference that Bench was only 17 when he started his pro baseball career in the minors. He was a sensation, and his coaches and managers were astonished that such a young player could catch and throw so well—better, in fact, than many catchers already in the big leagues. Bench was so impressive that one minor league team (Peninsula) retired his number as soon as he was promoted to a team in a higher league. He made a successful major league debut at the end of 1967 after being named the Minor League Player of the Year while playing for Triple A Buffalo. A finger injury curtailed his playing time that September, a benefit in the sense that because of the injury Bench would have a full season the following year (and not just a handful of games) to compete for the National League Rookie of the Year Award. He did, in fact, win the award in 1968, and the following spring the great Ted Williams gave Johnny an autographed baseball that said, "To Johnny Bench, A Hall of Famer for sure."

Bench's career unfolded from there in storybook fashion. He quickly became recognized as the best catcher in the game, he won a total of 10 Gold Glove Awards, and when he retired, some people thought he had been the best catcher to ever play the game. He became a dangerous hitter, especially in the clutch, and displayed exceptional power, especially for someone playing his demanding position. He led the league in home runs in 1970 (45)

## DID YOU KNOW...

That Johnny Bench was an A student in school, and he graduated as the valedictorian of Binger (Oklahoma) High School?

and 1972 (40) and finished his career as the leading home-run hitter in Reds history with a total of 389 homers. When he retired, the 327 homers he had hit as a catcher was also a major league record. In addition, on the Reds' all-time batting list Bench ranks first in RBIs (1,376), second in extra-base hits (794) and total bases (3,644), fourth in runs scored (1,091) and doubles (381), and fifth in hits (2,048).

Among the many gifts that Johnny Bench brought to bear upon his profession was a supreme self-confidence. Some people found him arrogant, but Bench said of the attitude he called "inner conceit": "To be the best, you have to believe that you are the best." Bench's cockiness not only helped him, it was a contagion that spread throughout the team and helped turn the Cincinnati ballclub into the Big Red Machine that won six divisional championships, four National League pennants, and two World Series, all in a single decade. That same confidence enabled Bench to take up a number of highly public sideline vocations, such as singing, acting, broadcasting, and serving as a corporate spokesperson, many of which he is still involved in today.

Bench continued to receive awards and honors after he retired from baseball. Two years after the Reds retired his uniform number, Bench was elected to the Reds Hall of Fame, a prelude to his being elected on the first try to the National Baseball Hall of Fame in 1989, along with Carl Yastrzemski. Johnny continues to live in Cincinnati, his adopted hometown, where he performs notable public services, such as financing a total renovation and upgrading of the University of Cincinnati's intercollegiate baseball facility, and where he continues to enjoy his status as one of the two or three most popular players to ever wear the uniform of the Cincinnati Reds.

## No. 20 Frank Robinson (May 22, 1998)

When the Reds retired No. 20, it wasn't just a ceremony honoring a great player. It was the extension by the ballclub and the acceptance of an olive branch by a player who been estranged from the franchise ever since his trade to the Baltimore Orioles, considered by most Reds fans to be the worst trade in team history.

Frank Robinson signed with the Cincinnati Reds right out of McClymonds High School in Oakland, California, where he had been a basketball teammate of Boston Celtics great Bill Russell. Robinson made his major league debut as a 20-year-old with a sensational season that netted him the first unanimous Rookie of the Year Award in either league. He made the All-Star team that year and hit 38 home runs to tie the National League record for homers by a rookie. He also led the league in hit-by-pitches (20)—something he would do six times in his Reds career—because he crowded the plate fearlessly and refused to be intimidated by pitchers who threw at him. Eventually, National League pitchers, afraid of his bat and unable to scare him, began pitching around him in tight spots, and Robinson led the league in intentional passes four years in a row (1961–1964).

Trading Frank Robinson and his "old body" to the Baltimore Orioles turned out to be a disastrous move for the Reds.

Robinson was also a very aggressive base runner and a hard slider, who neither asked for nor gave any quarter. He was a good outfielder whose only weakness was a throwing arm that was merely adequate. Nevertheless, he was recognized as the team's unquestioned leader his entire Reds career, made five more NL All-Star teams, and won the 1961 NL MVP Award for leading the Reds to their unexpected pennant.

Reds officials always insisted that his ill-advised trade to Baltimore was strictly a baseball decision. The Reds' general manager at the time, Bill DeWitt, made the most infamous statement in Reds history in defending the trade: "Robinson is an old 30; he has an old body." Robinson thought the trade had nothing to do with baseball. He had faced racial prejudice not only during his minor league career, but also from the home team fans in Cincinnati who had begun to blame him for the ballclub's inability to win another pennant. The tipping point came when Robinson was arrested on a concealed weapon charge that occurred when he defended himself from a couple of menacing rednecks by brandishing—but not discharging—a pistol.

Robinson, of course, had the last laugh. Cincinnati benefited little from the trade, while Robinson turned a good Orioles team into a great one. In his very first year (1966) he led Baltimore to a World Series championship and won the American League Triple Crown (.316, 49, 122) and AL MVP Award, giving him the distinction of being the only player in history to win MVP awards in both leagues. Ironically, four years later he helped the Orioles win another World Series title, this time over his former team, the Reds. Robby hit two home runs and drove in four runs during the Series. He wound down his playing career with the Dodgers, Angels, and Indians, and with Cleveland in 1975 he became the first black manager in Major League Baseball history. His long career as a manager included stints with the San Francisco Giants, the Baltimore Orioles, and the Montreal Expos/Washington Nationals.

When he retired, Robinson ranked fourth on the all-time home-run list with 586 homers, behind only Hank Aaron, Babe Ruth, and Willie Mays. And even though his career in Cincinnati lasted only 10 years, he still holds many Reds batting records and ranks second among all Reds players in home runs (324) and fourth in RBIs (1,009), runs (1,043), and extra-base hits (692). He was elected to the Reds Hall of Fame in 1978 and to the National Baseball Hall of Fame in 1982.

## No. 8 Joe Morgan (June 6, 1998)

Joe Morgan played even fewer years in Cincinnati than Robinson had played, but in those eight years "Little Joe" transformed himself from a good player into a great one. Morgan, who had never batted .300 in seven years with the Houston Astros, became a star after he came to the Reds in the big three-for-five player swap with the Astros at the end of 1971.

Morgan immediately befriended Pete Rose. Drunk on the winning atmosphere that permeated the Reds clubhouse, the two baseball-holics lockered next to each other, supported each other, and picked each other's brains for information that could provide the slightest edge over the opposition. Morgan blossomed in his first year with the club, batting .292 (his highest mark so far in the big leagues) with 16 home runs and 73 RBIs, while leading the league in walks (115), runs (122), and on-base percentage (.417). He finished fourth in the NL MVP Award voting, and it was all just a prelude of the excellence to come.

During his time in Cincinnati, Morgan was the catalyst of the Reds offense, as well as the scourge of National League pitchers. If you pitched to him, he was a threat to hit the ball out of the park. If you walked him or even held him to a single, he was such a threat to steal that it was like putting a man on second base to start with. Morgan compiled an on-base percentage of over .400 for five more consecutive years, and he led the league in on-base

## FAST FACTS

Second baseman Joe Morgan (1972–1979) was only 5'7" tall, but he was a giant of a player. Morgan led the Reds in stolen bases six years in a row and was National League MVP in 1975 and 1976.

Second baseman Joe Morgan's arrival from the Houston Astros transformed the Reds from a good team into the Big Red Machine.

percentage from 1974 to 1976, with marks of .427, .466, and .444. He put together the best years of his career in 1975 and 1976 in leading the team to the two World Series wins that certified the Big Red Machine as one of the greatest assemblages of baseball talent in baseball history. In 1975 Joe stole 67 bases and batted .327 with 17 homers and 94 RBIs; in 1976 he pilfered 60 bases and batted .320 with 27 homers and 111 RBIs. Morgan made the NL All-Star team all eight years he spent in Cincinnati, and he won the NL Gold Glove Award for second baseman five straight years (1973–1977). All in all, Joe's career with the Reds was a display of talent, versatility, and leadership seldom ever seen before in the major leagues.

Morgan left Cincinnati after the 1979 season as a free agent and finished out his career with the Astros, San Francisco Giants, Philadelphia Phillies, and Oakland A's. He remains the Reds' all-time champion base stealer (406), and he ranks third, behind Jeff Kent and Ryne Sandberg, in career home runs by second basemen with 268. Today he runs a number of successful businesses and has become a popular and instructive baseball color analyst. He was elected to the Reds Hall of Fame in 1987 and to the National Baseball Hall of Fame in 1990.

# REDS GOLD GLOVE WINNERS BEFORE AND AFTER THE BIG RED MACHINE

Think the Big Red Machine played good defense? According to the results of the Gold Glove Award voting, they certainly did. One way we can get some idea of how slick with the leather the players of the Big Red Machine era were is to compare the number of Gold Gloves they won with the number won by Reds players in all other years.

For the purposes of this comparison, we will consider the years from 1968, when a Big Red Machine player (Johnny Bench) first won a Gold Glove, to 1979, the year for which the final Gold Glove won by a Big Red Machine player (Dave Concepcion) was awarded, to be the Big Red Machine era. In that 12-year period, Reds players won a total of 28 Gold Gloves. In the 39 years before and since the Big Red Machine era, Reds players have won 18 Gold Gloves.

The most Gold Gloves won by a Reds player not a member of the Big Red Machine is three, a mark shared by shortstop Roy McMillan, outfielder Eric Davis, and shortstop Barry Larkin. McMillan was the first Red to win a Gold Glove, and he had the honor of being on the first Gold Glove team in history in 1957, when only one player from the two leagues combined was selected for each position. The Reds have never placed more than one member at a time on the NL Gold Glove team with the exception of 1958 and the Big Red Machine years, when the Reds had multiple Gold Glove winners eight times.

1957 Roy McMillan

1958 Roy McMillan, Frank
    Robinson, Harvey Haddix

1959 Roy McMillan

1961 Vada Pinson

1963 Johnny Edwards

1964 Johnny Edwards

1965 Leo Cardenas

1987 Eric Davis

1988 Eric Davis

1989 Eric Davis

1994 Barry Larkin

1995 Barry Larkin

1996 Barry Larkin

1998 Bret Boone

1999 Pokey Reese

2000 Pokey Reese

## No. 18 Ted Kluszewski (July 18, 1998)

When a sportswriter asked New York Giants manager Leo Durocher who he thought was the strongest player in the National League, Durocher thought for a second and offered Dodgers first baseman Gil Hodges as his answer.

"What about Ted Kluszewski?" pressed the writer.

"Kluszewski?" shot back Durocher. "I thought we were talking about human beings!"

Durocher's categorization of Kluszewski as a member of a different species may have been facetious, but it also wasn't that far off from the image that the rest of the world always had of the Reds' big first baseman. Kluszewski was a Hercules in spikes and flannel knickers, and photographers loved to take pictures of him holding a pile of bats fanned out in front of himself as if they were mere sticks, his huge biceps bulging and free of the cutoff uniform sleeves that were simply too confining.

A Big Ten football star, Ted Kluszewski was so big and so strong he might have played professional football instead of professional baseball. Then again, he probably made the right career choice, judging by the way things turned out and given the fact that the reason he decided to play baseball, his third favorite sport in high school, at Indiana University in the first place was to get out of participating in spring football practice.

"Big Klu," as he was known, hit .429 as a sophomore at IU, yet he was discovered by a Reds groundskeeper, not a Reds scout. (Lefty Gomez joked that Kluszewski had not been scouted, but trapped.) Because of travel restrictions imposed on major league teams during World War II, the Reds conducted their 1945 spring training on Indiana's campus in Bloomington. One day Kluszewski helped get the field ready for the Reds, and as a reward for his hard work the Reds groundskeeper arranged for him to take some swings during batting practice. When Ted began cracking long drives that would have easily flown out of Crosley Field, the Reds realized that they had stumbled onto a can't-miss major league prospect.

Kluszewski blistered the pitching he faced during two stops in the minors, hitting .352 for Columbia, South Carolina, in the Sally League and .377 for Memphis in the Southern Association.

He made his major league debut (10 at-bats in nine games) with the Reds at the end of 1947 at the age of 22 and turned in a respectable rookie year in 1948, batting .274 with 12 home runs in 113 games. He was not a home-run terror right away, as his high for a season was 25 homers (in 1950) over the first five years of his career. Of course, once he found the range, Klu did rack up big totals, averaging 43 home runs and 116 RBIs a year over a four-year period (1953–1956). These numbers, and especially his peak totals of 49 and 141, both of which led the National League in 1954, were honest ones, compiled without the aid of performance-enhancing drugs. When Klu cracked those 49 homers, only six other players had ever hit more, and 49 would remain the franchise record until George Foster hit 52 in 1977.

Home runs and big muscles were not the whole Ted Kluszewski story, though. He was a consistently good hitter, not a one-dimensional free-swinging slugger, and he batted over .300 five straight seasons. His low strikeout totals would have made a singles hitter half his size proud, and after a lot of dedicated practice he became a smooth enough glove man to lead National League first basemen in fielding five consecutive years. In other words, Big Klu could do everything except run and sing the national anthem.

The best thing of all about Kluszewski was the man himself, humble, gentle, and friendly to one and all. With his size and palpable strength, Kluszewski could have intimidated practically everyone he came into contact with. He chose to do otherwise. Reds beat writer Earl Lawson could be quite critical of the players

## DID YOU KNOW...

That Ted Kluszewski (1947–1957) felt constrained by his Reds baseball jerseys, so to give the bulging muscles in his arms more freedom he cut off his shirt sleeves? The Reds later adopted the look for the entire team, thus inventing the sleeve-less baseball jersey style.

at times, and Kluszewski had an appropriate nickname for him: "Poison Pen." "Thankfully," Lawson said after he'd retired, "Ted was always smiling when he called me that."

Opposing players, too, appreciated Klu's restraint and knew better than to physically challenge him. While running out a ground ball, scrappy Eddie Stanky of the Giants once collided with Kluszewski at first base. The collision knocked Stanky down 15 feet from the bag. Stanky clambered to his feet and then rushed up to Klu. "The fans in the Polo Grounds let out a big roar because they thought I was running up to fight Kluszewski," said Stanky, "but I wasn't crazy enough to do that. I just wanted to ask him if he was okay."

One day when a fight broke out between the Reds and the Cardinals, another feisty player, the St. Louis second baseman Solly Hemus, rushed out of the Cardinals' dugout to join the fray. Moments later Hemus felt himself suspended off the ground, his legs churning futilely in the air like a cartoon character. "Where do you think you're going, Solly?" said the bear of a man holding Hemus. "Nowhere, Ted, nowhere," said Hemus.

Even off the diamond and away from the spotlight, Kluszewski treated people the right way. Longtime Cincinnati Reds fan Wally Herbert remembers what happened one day when his father, a plumber, took him along on a job to the Kluszewskis, who were having a room added onto their home. "My dad and his helpers were digging a trench for the water lines in the backyard, and Kluszewski came out of the house to shoot the breeze with them," says Herbert. "We were thrilled that he'd come out of the house at all, and he couldn't have been nicer to everybody. But then his wife, Eleanor, opened a window and shouted, 'Theodore! Don't just stand there gabbing. Get down there and help those men dig. It will be good for your back.'

"We couldn't believe it, but Kluszewski did just like she'd said: he jumped down into the trench and helped my dad and the other guys do the work he was paying them to do."

The rehabilitative need referred to by Eleanor Kluszewski was caused by the only serious injury Kluszewski ever suffered, a slipped disc in his lower back. It effectively brought his career to

Home-run hitter Ted Kluszewski was a giant among men for the Reds in the 1950s.

a premature end, a demise initiated with the trade in December of 1957 that sent Kluszewski to the Pirates for fellow first baseman Dee Fondy. Kluszewski, who finished his career with 279 home runs, 1,766 hits, and a .298 batting average, enjoyed a last hurrah with the Chicago White Sox, slugging three home runs for the Pale Hose in the 1959 World Series against the Dodgers. Kluszewski later served as the Reds' hitting instructor, and players up and down the rosters of Reds teams in the 1970s and 1980s credited him with increasing their confidence and helping them to refine their batting strokes.

Even the pitchers on those teams loved Big Klu. Pitchers such as reliever Brad Lesley, who moved to Japan for 10 years to pitch and afterwards to work as an interpreter and sports announcer. "During that time I only came back to the States twice...for two funerals," says Lesley. "One was for my mom; the other one was for Ted Kluszewski."

## No. 24 Tony Perez (May 27, 2000)

A native Cuban, Tony Perez left a job in a Havana sugar cane factory to sign with the Cincinnati Reds. He overcame his shyness and inability to speak English to become one of the four pillars (along with Pete Rose, Johnny Bench, and Joe Morgan) of the dynasty erected by the Reds in the 1970s, as well as one of the most popular players in franchise history. Perez is also remembered as the player whose trade to the Montreal Expos after the Reds had won the 1976 World Series signaled the beginning of the unraveling of that dynasty.

Perez started slowly, as a part-time first baseman, but became the Reds' regular third baseman in his fourth season (1967), when he batted .290 with 26 home runs and 102 RBIs. He guarded the hot corner for the next four seasons, displaying a strong and accurate arm, before crossing the diamond to become the regular first baseman, the position he played for the rest of his career. Tony had his best season in 1970 when he notched career highs in batting average (.317), home runs (40), and RBIs (129). While other Reds players garnered more attention for doing flashy things, Perez earned everyone's respect for plodding away and consistently driving in runs—he drove in 90 or more runs for 10 consecutive seasons for the Reds, and his 1,028 RBIs during the 10-year stretch of 1967–1976 led all major league batters. Nicknamed "Big Doggie" for his ability to drive in runs, Tony also demonstrated a penchant for coming up with the big hit. His home run off Catfish Hunter in the fifteenth inning won the 1967 All-Star Game (and earned him the game's MVP award), and his three home runs were crucial in the Reds' victory over the Boston Red Sox in the 1975 World Series.

It didn't take long for the Reds to realize that trading the 34-year-old Perez was a colossal blunder. His replacement in the lineup, the 25-year-old Dan Driessen, never hit the way the Reds thought he would, but it was Perez's leadership and clubhouse presence that was missed the most. Perez had always helped the younger Spanish-speaking kids on the team, who looked up to him as a big-brother figure, and Tony served as a buffer between the big egos on the team, his wit and playful nature able to raise spirits after tough losses and able to diffuse moments of anger before they boiled over into something serious. Years later the man who traded Perez admitted the mistake. "Losing Tony took so much chemistry away," said former Reds GM Bob Howsam. "He had more of an effect on our team—on and off the field—than I ever realized."

Seven years after leaving, Perez came back to Cincinnati to finish out his career while playing for his old buddy, manager Pete Rose. On the next-to-last day of his final season (1986), he hit his 379th home run to tie him with Orlando Cepeda for most career home runs hit by a Latin American player. The seven-time NL All-Star ranks among the Reds' all-time leaders in RBIs (second), home runs (third), total bases (fourth), extra-base hits (fifth), games (sixth), at-bats (sixth), hits (sixth), and doubles (sixth). Tony was elected to the Reds Hall of Fame in August of 1998, and he was finally elected, after years of disappointment, to the National Baseball Hall of Fame in 2000. He was inducted into Cooperstown's shrine on July 23, 2000, along with Reds manager Sparky Anderson and dead-ball era Reds second baseman Bid McPhee. Perez managed the Reds briefly in 1993, and his son Eduardo also played in the major leagues.

## No. 10 Sparky Anderson (May 28, 2005)

When GM Bob Howsam hired Sparky Anderson to manage the Reds on October 9, 1969, the headlines in the Cincinnati newspapers screamed, "Sparky WHO?" When Howsam's replacement Dick Wagner fired Anderson a decade later, the same papers and Reds fans everywhere were outraged.

Cincinnati's unfamiliarity with Anderson was understandable. Anderson had spent his life in baseball, but he had pretty much flown under the radar. Anderson, who never did attend college, began his baseball education at the feet of a master, serving as batboy for the University of Southern California Trojans, coached by the legendary Rod Dedeaux. He attracted the attention of base-ball scouts when the American Legion team he played on won the National Championship in 1951—it helped that the final game took place in Tiger Stadium (named Briggs Stadium at the time). Anderson struggled as a weak-hitting second baseman for six years

**Johnny Bench, Tony Perez, Joe Morgan, and Sparky Anderson (left to right) have all had their numbers retired by the Reds.** (Photo courtesy of Getty Images.)

in the Dodgers' farm system before he got his chance in the majors, which lasted exactly one season. He played in 152 games for the 1959 Philadelphia Phillies and batted .218 with 12 extra-base hits and 34 RBIs. He played out the string with Toronto for four years, never hitting above .257, before beginning his managing career.

Anderson hardly set the world on fire at the beginning of his minor league managing career. He was a hothead and too impatient with both his players and the umpires. In 1965 he found himself out of baseball and looking at a future of selling cars when Howsam, with St. Louis at the time, needed a manager at the last minute for a team at the bottom of the Cardinals' minor league system. Howsam's right-hand man, Chief Bender, had seen Anderson's explosive temper on display during a ballgame in Jacksonville, Florida, and tried, unsuccessfully, to dissuade Howsam from hiring him. Sparky was too anxious to get back into baseball to even notice the negative way Bender presented the job offer. As reported by Greg Rhodes in *Big Red Dynasty*, the conversation, sans negotiating, went as follows:

> "Sparky, we have an opening. I don't know if you'd be interested."
>
> "I'll take it."
>
> "Sparky, it's only a Class D ballclub in South Carolina."
>
> "It don't matter. I'll take it."
>
> "Sparky, I haven't even mentioned salary to you."
>
> "I don't care. Pay me what you want. I'll take it."

Anderson proved that Howsam's instincts about him being good managerial material were correct, and he even learned to get his temper under control, thanks in large part to an altercation with an umpire that year. After the ump bumped into him during a heated argument, Anderson grabbed the arbiter and tried to throw him to the ground before cooler heads intervened and hustled him into the clubhouse. Fearing that his career was then over, Anderson was relieved and grateful when the umpire took part of the blame and promised to report only Anderson's bad language as the cause of his ejection from the game. Anderson's trademark habit of stuffing his hands into his back pockets when going out to argue with umpires stemmed from the incident.

Howsam later hired Anderson in 1968 to manage the Reds' minor league team in Asheville, North Carolina. Sparky served as a coach for the San Diego Padres in 1969 and was preparing to coach for the California Angels in 1970 when Howsam came calling with the job of managing the Reds.

Though his silver hair made him look much older, Anderson was only 35 years old when he took the Reds job. He surrounded himself with coaches who were experienced baseball men and old friends and won over everyone with his folksy charm, relentless optimism, and English-mangling, Stengel-like way of expressing himself. He also won, while always giving credit to the players: five divisional titles, four pennants, and two World Series championships in nine years. The Reds were talented ballclubs in those years, to be sure, but Anderson made indispensable contributions. His psychological acumen enabled him to instill confidence in key young players (such as Dave Concepcion); his thorough preparation and velvet-gloved discipline maintained a winning atmosphere; and his extensive and frequent use of the bullpen not only earned him the sobriquet Captain Hook, but also heralded the age of relief pitching specialization that is universally in effect today. When told that he was being dismissed, after two second-place finishes in a row, because the Reds "wanted to go in a different direction," Anderson asked Wagner, "Where do you want to go? The moon?"

Sparky, of course, didn't stay unemployed for long. Detroit hired him a third of the way through the 1979 season, and exactly five full seasons later he led the Tigers to the 1984 World Series title, after they got off to a record 35–5 start. With that championship Anderson became the first manager to win 100 games in a season and the first to win a World Series with teams in both leagues. He was also named Manager of the Year in both leagues. With 2,194 wins, he ranks fifth among all major league managers. His 1975 and 1976 World Series champs combined to go 210–114 (.648), and he is the Reds' all-time leader in victories (863) and

# REDS ALL-20ᵀᴴ-CENTURY TEAM

An All-20ᵗʰ-Century Reds team has not been officially picked, but if Reds fans were asked to choose such a team, here is what I think it would look like. This lineup is quite different from the All-Time Reds Team that the fans selected in 1969. There are three things to note about this new team: first, the replacement of players on the 1969 team by members of the Big Red Machine at five positions: catcher, left field, first base, second base, and third base; second, the retention of Bucky Walters and Eppa Rixey, an indication of the organization's continuing failures and just plain bad luck in the pitching department; and finally, the displaced player from the 1969 team with the strongest argument for not being displaced is third baseman Heinie Groh. He actually had a more outstanding career at third base than Pete Rose, but Rose must be on the team somewhere. You might want to retain Groh at third and put Rose on the team as the left fielder, which would certainly be a reasonable option. What it boils down to is who you would rather have on the team, Groh or George Foster. Obviously, I would take Foster's power over Groh's average. Ken Griffey Jr. and Eric Davis received strong consideration, but neither of them really deserved to unseat the player at his position based on the players' careers with Cincinnati. The closest thing to a toss-up would be at shortstop: Larkin or Dave Concepcion? Take your pick.

First base—Tony Perez
Second base—Joe Morgan
Third base—Pete Rose
Shortstop—Barry Larkin
Right field—Frank Robinson
Center field—Edd Roush
Left field—George Foster
Catcher—Johnny Bench
Right-handed pitcher—Bucky Walters
Left-handed pitcher—Eppa Rixey

winning percentage (.596). He was elected to the Reds Hall of
Fame on June 3, 2000, and to the National Baseball Hall of Fame
in Cooperstown in August of 2000 along with one of his favorite
former players, Tony Perez.

## No. 13 Dave Concepcion (August 25, 2007)

Although Dave Concepcion ranks behind the big four of the Big
Red Machine, he was an important, indeed an essential, part of the
team's success. The Big Red Machine is remembered as an offensive
powerhouse, but many a slug-happy team has won nothing more
than accolades. The Reds' pitching in the 1970s was always better
than a lot of people realized, and the defense was as good as the
offense. The Reds had strength up the middle (catcher, shortstop,
second base, and center field), and Concepcion was the cornerstone of that strength behind the pitcher's mound.

A native of Aragua, Venezuela, Concepcion was a scrawny kid
when he began his pro career as a second baseman with the Reds'
rookie league team in Tampa. Noticing the kid's arm and fluidity,
George Scherger switched him to short, and Concepcion arrived
in the big leagues after playing only 258 games in the minors, 42
of them at Triple A Indianapolis. Against the advice of his super-
stitious teammates, he requested No. 13 for his uniform jersey
because his mother had been born in 1913. A weak stick at first,
Concepcion made himself into a hitter by carefully listening to
his teammates, who were always discussing the art, and by
working with hitting coach Ted Kluszewski, who made David a
special project.

After three years of part-time play, Concepcion became the
Reds' starting shortstop in 1973. He made the National League
All-Star team that year, then on July 22 suffered a broken ankle,
which ended his season. He led the NL in fielding average in 1977
and won five Gold Gloves (1974–1977 and 1979) for his fielding
excellence. When he hit .301 in 1978, it was the first time a Reds
shortstop had hit .300 since Joe Tinker in 1913. Davey made the
NL All-Star team eight more times in a row (1975–1982), and he
was named the MVP of the 1982 game for hitting a game-winning
home run against Dennis Eckersley of the Boston Red Sox.

Concepcion hurt his elbow in 1980 and began throwing the ball to first on one bounce. Designed to take stress off his arm, the one-hop throw became another technique in Concepcion's fielding bag of tricks when he realized that the ball actually got there faster on the bounce off artificial turf. In recognition of his leadership the Reds named Concepcion captain in 1983, making him the first captain of the team since Sparky Anderson had named Pete Rose captain in 1970. David won a pair of Silver Slugger Awards as the best hitting shortstop in the league in 1981 and 1982, and in 1977 he won the Roberto Clemente Award as the top Latin American ballplayer. He helped groom Barry Larkin as his replacement and retired in 1988, after having spent his entire 19-year career with the Reds. He was elected to the Reds Hall of Fame in 2000.

Although Cooperstown itself has yet to make the call to Dave Concepcion, many experts believe he is more than qualified for election to the National Baseball Hall of Fame. "I guarantee you Davey is as good as Pee Wee Reese and Phil Rizzuto," Pete Rose has said. "Davey was a better all-around player than Ozzie Smith. Not as good defensively, but offensively he was better." Pee Wee Reese himself, one of the two shortstops already in the Hall of Fame whom Rose alluded to, was also one of Concepcion's admirers. In comparing Davey to the other top shortstops of the 1970s, Reese said, "Mark Belanger may be a little smoother. Larry Bowa is very quick. Rick Burleson is a leader type. Bill Russell has an accurate arm. But no one does everything as well as Concepcion. It's possible no one ever has."

## No. 14 Pete Rose (unofficially, after the 1978, 1989, and 1997 seasons)

A public ceremony to honor the man and his number would be a mere formality, as Pete Rose's No. 14 is a retired Reds uniform number just as surely as any of the other numbers discussed in this chapter. Furthermore, if they were allowed to, the Reds would officially retire No. 14, even while Rose is denied the place in baseball's pantheon that he so clearly earned on the diamond. When Rose left Cincinnati for a bigger payday with the

Philadelphia Phillies after the 1978 season, clubhouse manager Bernie Stowe crossed No. 14 off the list of numbers available to Reds players. When Pete returned from exile (Montreal) in 1984, his old number was waiting for him to don again. Rose departed town for good in 1989, in disgrace and under suspicion, yet so great is the respect that the organization has for his accomplishments in a Reds uniform that No. 14 went back into the closet. Fourteen was Lou Piniella's number, yet even as the manager of the team he was not given the number. (He reversed the numbers and wore No. 41 as Reds manager; he got to wear No. 14 again in 1993 went he became manager of the Seattle Mariners.)

There was only one circumstance that could have brought the number back into use, and it happened in 1997 when Pete Rose Jr. played briefly for the Cincinnati Reds and had the privilege of being the last Reds player to ever wear No. 14 on his back. No. 14 has not been issued by the Reds again, nor will it ever be issued, regardless of whether or not it is ever officially retired. Such is the due of players as great as Pete Rose.

# REDS CULTURE

The Cincinnati Reds are more than just a professional sports team. To the citizens of Cincinnati, the Reds are the city's security blanket, a maker of happy memories, and a boundless source of fascination, excitement, and civic pride. A few people at a time may actually hold the mortgage on the franchise, but in reality the Reds belong to the entire Queen City and to Reds fans in all parts of what is known as Reds country: most of Ohio, all of Kentucky, Southern Indiana, and even parts of West Virginia, Virginia, and Tennessee. Once every couple of decades or so, there is talk about the Reds relocating to a different city, but such a thing is a virtual impossibility and nobody ever takes such blustering seriously. If the Reds were ever to leave Cincinnati, the heart and soul of the place would follow and the going-out-of-business sale of the entire city would commence. Becoming a Reds fan is something that happens automatically to anybody born in Reds country. Cincinnati does not have two major league baseball teams that split the allegiance of its citizens, and when Reds fans move away from southern Ohio (or northern Kentucky or southwestern Indiana) they don't take up with the baseball team that is followed by the residents of their new city or town. If anything, transplanted Reds fans have the team's logo that has always been tattooed on their heart tattooed on their body somewhere. Yes, the Reds sometimes frustrate their fans—sometimes for years on

171

end—but those fans never turn in their loyalty cards. In fact, Reds fans love their team so much that they have found numerous ways to stay connected to the team, even when there is not a game underway to be watched. The widespread, never-ending interest in the team has produced a web of conversation, activities, contacts, and artifacts that Reds fans can plug into at any time to get their fix, and that conglomeration of things sustained by interest in the team is what we call Reds culture.

## THE REDS' LITERARY TRADITION

Xavier University students like to call their school, founded in Cincinnati in 1831, "the Harvard of the Midwest," but as one comic has noted, "I don't think Harvard's students are going around bragging that Harvard is 'the Xavier of the Northeast.'" While Cincinnati has never claimed to be the literary beacon that Boston is, when it comes to writing about baseball, the home of the Reds takes a backseat to no other town.

Although it is well-known that the Red Stockings of 1869 were baseball's first professional team, little is made of the equally noteworthy fact that Cincinnati supplied baseball's first beat writer: Harry Millar, who traveled with the Red Stockings on their historic eastern tour of '69. Millar worked for the *Cincinnati Commercial* and sent his dispatches back to the newspaper by telegraph. Three other Cincinnati papers assigned reporters to most of the Red Stockings' local matches, and their coverage, combined with Millar's, kept Cincinnatians amazingly well-informed about the glorious strivings of the Red Stockings at a time when the newspaper sports section as we know it today did not exist. In addition to being the granddaddy of all baseball beat writers, Millar deserves some of the credit for helping to establish the viability of the professional game by keeping the underfunded Red Stockings alive at the beginning of their tour. When club officials outlined the team's dire money situation to him after a game in Yellow Springs, Ohio, Millar lent the club $245 of his own expense allotment, which he was later repaid in New York.

Millar is hardly the only Cincinnati sportswriter to make a mark on the national pastime. O.P. Caylor, a baseball writer for the *Cincinnati Enquirer* who was also the most famous baseball writer of the day when the Reds got kicked out of the National League in late 1880, helped organize a rival league, the American Association, which the Reds promptly joined. Four years later, Caylor walked away from his typewriter, took the helm of the team, and skippered the Reds to second- and fifth-place finishes for the 1885 and 1886 seasons, respectively. No less a luminary than Ban Johnson, the founder of the American League, got his start in baseball as the sports editor of the *Cincinnati Commercial-Gazette*. Although James C. Isaminger gained prominence for his long career with Philadelphia papers, he broke into the business with the *Cincinnati Times-Herald*. Isaminger was second only to Hugh Fullerton in uncovering the Black Sox scandal; he edited the Reach Guides for more than a decade; and he was voted into the writers' wing of the Baseball Hall of Fame in 1974. Tom Swope joined the *Cincinnati Post* in 1915 and covered the Reds for 41 years. In 1949 he was named to a committee to revise the rules for scoring and wound up doing most of the writing for the revisions. Owner of a pet monkey and alligator, Bill Phelon, a baseball writer for the *Cincinnati Times-Star,* was as flaky as any of the ballplayers he ever covered. Before he died, Phelon arranged for his ashes to be sent to an old drinking buddy in Cuba with instructions for the ashes to be sprinkled solemnly over picturesque Morro Castle, which stands guard over the entrance to Havana Bay. In remembrance of Phelon, the drinking buddy took the ashes with him on a farewell pub crawl, but woke up the next morning with a hangover and no memory of what had become of his friend's last remains. Jack Ryder, who had a long and distinguished career with the *Enquirer,* was one of the three writers at the Detroit–Chicago World Series of 1935 who were instrumental in organizing the Baseball Writers Association of America. Other princes of the press box in Cincinnati were Lou Smith, Pat Harmon, Earl Lawson, Ritter Collett, and Si Burick. The present-day dean of the Cincinnati pressbox is the affable, cigar-chomping Hal McCoy of

# TOP 10 NICKNAMES OF 1961 REDS AS FOUND IN JIM BROSNAN'S *PENNANT RACE*

"The Professor"—The team's nickname for Brosnan, whose love of classical music, pipe smoking, and reading made him seem like an intellectual to his teammates. The witty reliever was also known as "Broz," "Fess" (short for Professor), and "Captain" (because he supposedly had the highest rank of anyone in the Reds' bullpen).

"Gabby"—A facetious moniker for reliever Bill Henry because he was the exact opposite of talkative.

"Tits"—Hung on starting pitcher Jim Maloney for a pronounced part of his anatomy.

"The Colonel"—Coach Jim Turner's authoritative manner earned him this sobriquet.

"The Sherriff"—A play on the first name of relief pitcher Marshall Bridges. Bridges liked to refer to himself as "The Fox," for his supposed craftiness on the mound.

"The Apache"—The boys in the bullpen stuck this nickname on bespeckled reliever Howie Nunn for his habit of wearing a thick white sweatband around his head.

"Tootie"—An affectionate corruption of starting pitcher Jim O'Toole's surname.

"Blazer"—Derived from the sound of second baseman Don Blasingame's name, as well as a reference to his foot speed.

"Augie"—When Reds third baseman Gene Freese was a rookie with the Dodgers, Brooklyn's PA announcer Tex Rickards didn't know his first name. As a joke, Freese's teammates said that his name was "Augie"...the same as the umpire (Augie Donatelli) who was scheduled to work the plate that day.

"Roadblock"—Pitcher Sherman Jones got this nickname in the minors when a sportswriter wrote that Jones's pitching amounted to a roadblock against the opponents' efforts to score. The Reds often called Jones "Road" for short.

the *Dayton Daily News*. Everyone's confidant and an unscoopable reporter, McCoy has continued to work flawlessly despite losing his eyesight. His fame has been assured, as he, too, is already a recipient of the J.G. Taylor Spink Award. Burick, Lawson, and Collett also won the award, giving small-market Cincinnati an impressive total of four Hall of Fame sportswriters who spent their entire careers covering the Reds.

The first baseball magazine devoted to baseball poetry and fiction, *Spitball: The Literary Baseball Magazine,* was founded by yours truly in 1981 in Reds country, in Covington, Kentucky. The magazine, which sponsors the oldest and most prestigious honor for baseball books, the Casey Award, moved its offices across the Ohio River to Cincinnati in the fall of 1986 in order to be based in the same city where professional baseball started. All facets of the Reds and of the ballclub's minor league farm system receive extensive coverage from an independent monthly newspaper called *Reds Report.* The paper began in Cincinnati (under a different name) in the 1980s, was later acquired by Coman Publishers in North Carolina, and today is published by Columbus Sports Publications in Columbus, Ohio.

Equally impressive is Cincinnati's contribution to the baseball book world, which began with a trio of very early Reds-related volumes. *In Memoriam: Aaron Burt Champion* was the first baseball biography ever published. This thin and exceedingly rare book about the man who served as the president of the Red Stockings from 1867 through 1870 was published in 1896, four years before the publication of Cap Anson's *A Ballplayer's Career,* the book often mistakenly described as the first baseball biography. Also extremely rare, *The Garry* is a book of newspaper cartoons about August "Garry" Herrmann, the president of the Reds from 1902 to 1927. Herrmann was prominent in Cincinnati politics, and the very unusual book bearing his name is both a review of the Reds' 1904 season and an often humorous profile of the man himself. More common but still rare enough to command a price of more than $1,000, *Baseball in Cincinnati* by Harry Ellard is one of the earliest team histories ever published. Ellard does cover the professional

# TOP 10 20ᵀᴴ-CENTURY REDS NICKNAMES (OTHER THAN THOSE USED IN *PENNANT RACE*)

1. "Charlie Hustle"—A great nickname for a great player: Pete Rose. Mickey Mantle and Whitey Ford came up with the name and meant it as an insult for a player they thought was faking excessive effort, but Rose proved over his long career that the name was a perfect description of the way he played the game. Later, writers used the nickname ironically in reference to Rose's gambling habits, tax troubles, and association with criminals.

2. "Captain Hook"—Given to manager Sparky Anderson for his propensity to yank starting pitchers at the first sign of trouble.

3. "The Whip"—Ewell Blackwell: because of the lanky right-hander's intimidating side-armed delivery, which reminded people of a buggy whip.

4. "Spuds"—With his burr haircut and goggles, third baseman Chris Sabo resembled the star of a popular beer commercial: a pooch named Spuds MacKenzie.

5. "The Animal"—One day while covering first base, relief pitcher Brad Lesley scared Johnny Bench to death, screaming at Bench to throw him the ball. Bench said afterward that Lesley looked like a wild animal on the play.

6. "Noodles"—Early 20ᵗʰ-century strikeout artist Frank George Hahn got his nickname as a boy, when neighbors saw the lad toting the same lunch every day to his father working at a piano factory: noodle soup.

7. "Schnozz"—An oh-so-clever reference to the big nose of Hall of Fame catcher Ernie Lombardi. As insensitive as "Dummy" Hoy's nickname, except that the deaf Hoy reputedly liked his nickname.

8. "Elmer"—Phillies shortstop Larry Bowa hung this nickname on his Reds counterpart, Dave Concepcion. One day Bowa asked Concepcion if his first name was "Elmer." The puzzled Concepcion said no and then asked Bowa why he would think such a thing. Bowa said, "Well, every day when I look at the Reds' box score in the paper, it says 'Concepcion—E'!"

9. "The Mayor of Riverfront"—Used to indicate the popularity of first baseman Sean Casey, who was universally well-liked.

10. "Nasty Boys"—A group nickname for a trio of Reds relievers: Randy Myers, Rob Dibble, and Norm Charlton. The three friends loved this nickname and even tried to capitalize on its popularity with things such as a poster and a rap song.

game and especially the exploits of the famous 1869–1970 Red Stockings, but he gives equal treatment to amateur baseball in Cincinnati, both prior to and after the advent of the Red Stockings. Those who know the city well are probably amazed and delighted to see Ellard discuss with all seriousness amateurs that hailed from Cincinnati neighborhoods such as Mount Auburn, College Hill, and Avondale, as well as from neighboring towns such as Newport and Ludlow, Kentucky.

In the late 1940s and early '50s, G.P. Putnams & Sons published a series of baseball team histories, and the volume on the Reds, published in 1948 and entitled *The Cincinnati Reds: An Informal History*, was written by Cincinnati native Lee Allen. The unathletic, rotund Allen grew up as a Crosley Field park rat who kept stats for the sportswriters in the press box while still attending Hughes High School (adjacent to the University of Cincinnati), and he wound up devoting his life to baseball research and history. Allen eventually became the first librarian at the National Baseball Library in Cooperstown, New York, and his vast knowledge of personal details about thousands of players became one of the Library's richest resources. He wrote a column for *The Sporting News* as well as several other highly regarded baseball books, but he remains best known as the author of the *Putnams Reds* history, a cornerstone volume in any library of books about the Reds.

The two most authentic books about the Reds, *The Long Season* and *Pennant Race*, were both written by the ultimate insider, pitcher Jim Brosnan, another Cincinnati native and an ex-Xavier student too cynical to exaggerate the university's ranking in academia. Nicknamed "The Professor" for his love of reading and classical music and his command of a decidedly supra-jock vocabulary, Brosnan often took notes in the bullpen and in the clubhouse. Before the publication of the first book in 1960, Broz's teammates were merely curious; as he worked on the second book, they were intent on being portrayed in a favorable light. Reds fans especially treasure *Pennant Race* because it chronicles the Reds' march to the 1961 National League flag in the face of widespread media skepticism, but both books provide as true a picture of major league baseball as one can find anywhere. And both books, full of great dialogue and inside baseball, are as entertaining today as they were when they burst upon the scene as radical departures from the usual baseball book fare. A few other players after Brosnan have written books without the help of coauthors, but none have ever matched *The Long Season* and *Pennant Race* in wit, insight, and literary quality.

The third baseman on the Reds' 1940 world championship team, Bill Werber, later achieved another impressive literary feat by penning his memoirs himself. Werber at first consented to being part of Lawrence Ritter's groundbreaking book of baseball oral histories, *The Glory of Their Times,* but later changed his mind when he became worried that his candid comments might adversely affect his insurance business. After Ritter's book became a smash hit and renewed the celebrity of the former players Ritter had interviewed for it, Werber changed his mind again and decided to write and publish his full-fledged autobiography. *Circling the Bases* is one of the few autobiographies written by a player of Werber's generation, and baseball bibliophiles are further drawn to it for its colorful red-and-green dust jacket featuring an illustration of the subject batting.

A steady stream of Reds biographies has been flowing since the 1960s, and to no one's surprise the king of this niche is the controversial Peter Edward Rose, a figure who has inspired equally tremendous amounts of admiration and disgust. At the height of Rose's popularity, the great Roger Kahn was called upon to write the definitive Rose biography, *Pete Rose: My Story,* which was published in 1989. As stylish as the writing in it is, Kahn's book turned out to be the definitive Rose apologia. A pair of well-documented, withering exposés by Michael Y. Sokolove (*Hustle: The Myth, Life, and Lies of Pete Rose,* 1990) and James Reston Jr. (*Collision at Home Plate: The Lives of Pete Rose and Bart Giamatti,* 1991) later revealed the ugly truths that Rose had managed to keep hidden from Kahn. Though he felt betrayed by his subject, Kahn maintained that he'd written the best book possible under the circumstances, and he took consolation in the fact that sales of the book surpassed 200,000 copies. The denial of his rightful place in Cooperstown continuing and costing him untold amounts of money, Rose himself later cashed in with an "as told to" confessional called *My Prison Without Bars.* It will hardly be the last word on Rose, as the hit king is as fascinating and as complex a figure as baseball has ever produced. Other notable Reds biographies include *Catch You Later* by Johnny Bench and William Brashler; *The Main Spark* by Sparky Anderson with Si Burick; *Marge Schott...Unleashed!* by Mike Bass; and the long-overdue Joe Nuxhall story, *Joe: Rounding Third and Heading for Home* by Greg Hoard, which appeared in 2005.

The modern classic of Reds literature is *The Cincinnati Game* by *Cincinnati Post* sportswriter Lonnie Wheeler. Jammed with wonderful anecdotes, trenchant observations, obscure tidbits of info, and eye-catching graphics, the book set a new standard for team histories that writers and designers have aspired to match ever since it appeared in 1988. The book is also hard to find, as only 3,000 hardbacks were printed, but the key to the book's appeal is its brash attitude that Cincinnati is, and always has been, the center of the baseball universe.

The man most responsible for keeping this Reds tradition of literary excellence going strong is the Reds' official historian and former director of the Reds Hall of Fame and Museum, Greg Rhodes, who, before taking the director's position, started his own publishing company for the express purpose of producing books about the team. With Road West Publishing we come full circle, as Rhodes's company made its debut in 1994 with *The First Boys of Summer,* the book which tells for the first time the complete, detailed story of baseball's first professional team. The 1869 Red Stockings were a good place to start, but Road West did not stop there; Rhodes has also published books on Crosley Field, the Big

Red Machine, and Opening Day, in addition to a big fat day-by-day and year-by-year reference of Reds history and a nostalgic book of black-and-white Reds photographs. Taken altogether, it's a most impressive record but exactly what you would expect to be generated by the team with the longest and in many respects the richest heritage in baseball.

# REDS COLLECTIBLES

Among the most loyal of all Reds followers are the collectors, those fans who enhance their enjoyment of the team and strengthen their feelings of being connected to it by acquiring all sorts of Reds souvenirs, ephemera, mementos, pieces of memorabilia, and collectibles. In fact, Reds collectibles are so numerous and ubiquitous that it is almost impossible to be a Reds fan without possessing at least a few of them, such as ticket stubs or programs or any number of items that were given away as freebies at a Reds game. But for the hard-core collectors, Reds collectibles are a serious hobby, if not a passionate obsession.

There are as many ways to be a Reds collector as there are Reds fans, and no two Reds collections are alike; however, there are three basic approaches to collecting. The first approach is to collect items connected to one's favorite player. The advantage to this approach is that it limits the number of items that a collector has to track down, while allowing him to concentrate on the harder-to-find collectibles. Without a doubt, the two most commonly collected Reds players are Pete Rose and Johnny Bench, and an astonishing number of items related to each player exists. For instance, there are so many Rose items to collect that in 1997 Chuck Lumb and two partners issued *The Almost Complete Pete Rose Checklist*, a 79-page magazine-sized, spiral-bound guide to more than 2,400 Pete Rose baseball cards, oddball items, and publications. Rose collectibles continue to appear, and it may be true, as the authors of *The Almost Complete Pete Rose Checklist* opined, that "Pete Rose has more collectibles than any baseball player before or since, including the immortal Babe Ruth." While Rose and Bench attract the most collectors, there are collectors devoted to other Reds players, the most popular being Ted Kluszewski, Frank Robinson, Vada Pinson, Tony Perez, Joe Morgan, Barry Larkin, and Ken Griffey Jr. Any Reds player that a fan takes a shine to is potentially the subject of a collection, and the proof of that is the somewhat mysterious Alaskan collector devoted to former Reds pitcher Joey Jay, who identifies himself simply as "The Jay Man." It is not so easy in Alaska to find artifacts connected to a Reds pitcher from the 1960s, and so "The Jay Man" periodically runs notices in collecting publications advertising his desire to purchase Joey Jay items.

A second method used by some Reds collectors is to focus on a certain type of item, such as baseball cards, autographs, programs and yearbooks, ticket stubs, bats, bobbleheads, photos, pennants, glassware, schedules, press pins, media guides, jerseys, artwork, coins and medallions, statues and figurines, caps, cereal boxes and other food packaging, advertising pieces, and on and on. The categories are practically endless, and there is some Reds fan somewhere who specializes in every conceivable type of Reds collectible. For example, Cynthia Blore of Vandalia, Ohio, collects Reds key chains. She has more than 150 different ones in her collection, enough to decorate her entire Christmas tree! Whether on baseballs, on paper items, or on some other type of surface (such as a plastic mini-batting helmet), player autographs are an ancient and very popular type of Reds item to collect because fans feel a strong personal connection to a player through possession of his signature.

Autographed Reds team baseballs are highly prized collectibles, especially those bearing the signatures of one of the franchise's championship squads. The single-signature Reds autographed baseball is most valuable when the signature appears on the ball's "sweet spot" and when the ball is a brand-new, "unrubbed-up" official National League baseball, not some cheaper substitute, such as a Little League– or high school–quality ball. Baseballs autographed by Reds who have been enshrined in Cooperstown command the highest prices, and according to *Tuff Stuff*'s guide to Hall of Fame autographs, the most valuable Reds signature is that of Red Stockings shortstop George Wright, worth about $8,500 on a baseball, followed by those of Eppa Rixey ($3,500), Ernie Lombardi ($1,400), and Edd Roush ($250). The relatively low value of Roush's signature is not a reflection of his stature as a player, but the result of his having lived such a long life—he died in 1988 at the age of 94—which gave fans a much greater than usual opportunity to obtain his autograph.

Many fans also collect game-used Reds equipment (bats, fielding gloves, batting helmets, catching gear) and game-worn uniforms (mainly jerseys and caps but also spikes and pants), which make wonderful display items in addition to providing the same strong personal connection as autographs. As a rule, the better the player, the greater value a game-used or game-worn item will have, but even items once belonging to ordinary players can be very valuable if the items date to periods of Reds history from which few such relics have survived. The most collectible of all Reds jerseys are those from the pre–double knit flannel era; jerseys from the Big Red Machine heyday years of 1975–1976; and the green Reds jerseys, which the Reds wore during spring training exhibition games on St. Patrick's Day for several years in the late 1970s and early 1980s. The latter jerseys are white with green lettering, numbers, trim, and Reds logos, and each sports a green shamrock patch on the left sleeve. The green jerseys were originally sold for about $50 a piece at the Reds' 580 Gift Shop in downtown Cincinnati but today are worth many times that initial price.

The third way for Reds collectors combines the first two approaches, and collecting a little bit of anything and everything Reds is what most Reds collectors actually do. While there are thousands of non–baseball card Reds items to be had for $20 or less, most collectors eventually graduate to the ranks of a higher class of collector who pursue the rarer and more expensive Reds items. Such a collector was Steve Cummings, who at one time owned one of the best and most valuable collections of Reds memorabilia in the world. Oddly, Cummings, a clinical psychologist who fell in love with the Reds as a kid while living in Boston, Massachusetts, listening to Reds games on the radio, put together his collection of Reds rarities while living in Seattle, Washington. Cummings's focus on rarities netted him treasures such as elaborately decorated

19th-century Reds scorecards, a silver complimentary season pass into the "Cincinnati Base Ball Park" for 1899, and a pair of oval bronze plaques bearing the likenesses of manager Pat Moran and team owner John Brush, which once hung inside Crosley Field. If anybody surpassed Cummings as a Reds collector, it was Barry Halper, whose massive accumulation of baseball treasures covering all teams and the entire length of baseball history rivaled the holdings of the National Baseball Hall of Fame and Museum in Cooperstown, New York. When Halper liquidated a large part of his collection during a weeklong auction by Sotheby's, the approximately 2,500 lots brought in almost $22 million. The Halper auction included more than 40 Reds items, the most expensive being the uniform that Pete Rose wore when he banged out hit number 4,192, which sold for $90,500. Believe it or not, that figure was only good for 18th place on the auction's list of most expensive items sold and was well behind the price rang up by the auction's crown jewel, the last ball glove used by Lou Gehrig, which fetched an astonishing $387,500. Eleven other vintage Reds jerseys were sold in the Halper auction, and while they did not approach the selling price of the uniform Rose wore when he passed Ty Cobb, they still put up some pretty good numbers: $19,500 (1968 Pete Rose road jersey), $7,475 (1947 Ewell Blackwell no-hit game home jersey), $3,220 (1955 Jim Greengrass home jersey), $2,900 (1969 Tony Perez home jersey), $2,587 (1976 George Foster road jersey), $2,300 (1971 Ted Kluszewski coach's road jersey), $2,300 (1949 Hank Sauer road jersey), $1,725 (1938 Kiddo Davis home jersey), $1,495 (1961 Joey Jay home jersey), $1,150 (1961 Dick Sisler home

# FAST FACTS

For several years in the late 1970s when the Reds held spring training in Tampa, Florida, the team wore uniforms that honored Cincinnati's Irish heritage during the exhibition games held on St. Patrick's Day. All parts of the uniform that were normally red were green, and a green shamrock adorned the left sleeve of each jersey.

coach's jersey), and $1,035 (1966 Gordy Coleman road jersey). The remaining Reds items in the Halper auction, representing an amazing range of rarities and treasures, did pretty well, too, as the following sample indicates: $40,250 (Pete Rose's 1973 Louisville Slugger silver batting champion bat), $17,250 (Heinie Groh's 1919 world championship diamond pin), $13,800 (an 1869 Red Stockings team card and schedule), $5,175 (an 1895 Opening Day complimentary pass to the game between Cincinnati and Cleveland), $2,587 (a Joe Morgan game-used bat), and $1,725 (an Edd Roush label cigar box).

Of course, a Reds collection does not have to be worth a fortune to bring an immense amount of enjoyment to its owner. For most Reds fans, the fun is in the collecting itself, in keeping a sharp eye out for the latest Reds souvenir to hit the market or for an obscure Reds artifact surfacing in a yard sale or estate auction. It also goes without saying that no Reds collection can be truly complete, as there are simply too many items for any one fan to own. Nevertheless, for Reds fans who aspire to own a collection that can hold its own with most any other, certain quality, fairly obtainable items should be considered essentials of Reds collecting, including the following classic pieces, all of recent vintage: a Crosley Field or Riverfront Stadium seat; a Big Red Machine art print, depicting a Reds slugger bopping the mascots of all the other National League teams and signed by famous baseball artist Willard Mullin; the metal serving tray decorated with a color team photo of the 1976 World Series champs that was produced and sold by the Reds; the Big Red Machine whiskey decanter in the shape of a catcher's mitt made in 1973 by Hoffman Distilling; a press pin from the Reds' 1978 tour of Japan, which features both the Reds' logo and a Japanese flag; ticket stubs from Johnny Bench retirement night, Rose's 4,192nd hit game, and any Reds World Series game; a pennant from the 1988 All-Star Game held at Riverfront; an Andy Warhol Pete Rose lithograph; authentic Hall of Fame press pins commemorating the inductions of Frank Robinson (1982), Ernie Lombardi (1986), Johnny Bench (1989), Joe Morgan (1990), and Tony Perez, Sparky Anderson, and Bid McPhee, who all went in together in 2000; a panoramic (five-foot long) color photo of Game 6 of the 1990 National League Championship Series between the Reds and the Pittsburgh Pirates, signed by photographer Brad LaPayne; a Crosley Field scoreboard desk clock by Pastimes; a limited edition (500), oversized 2000 Tony Perez Hall of Fame Induction commemorative pennant by

**This print depicting a Reds slugger smacking the mascots of the other National League teams makes a fine addition to any memorabilia collection.**
(Photo courtesy of Mike Shannon.)

# HAVING BREAKFAST WITH THE REDS

Since 1935, the General Mills cereal company has been supplying base-ball fans with wonderful collectibles, as American as reading the sports page at breakfast and as inexpensive as...well, a box of toasted wheat cereal flakes!

Wheaties, General Mills's most popular cereal, are tasty, nutritious, and connected in the public's mind with the best sports heroes our nation has produced. That's because Wheaties has been packaged over the years in boxes adorned with the images of great athletes and sports teams. While athletes from other sports have appeared on Wheaties boxes, baseball players have always been a Wheaties box staple. In earlier years, photos of baseball players were presented on the boxes in the style of baseball cards. For a couple of years (1936 and 1939) photos of the players were used to accentuate instructions on how to play the game, which were printed on the boxes. Today the Wheaties box appearance is primarily hon-orary in nature. World Series championships and Hall of Fame inductions are two baseball events almost guaranteed to be celebrated on a Wheaties

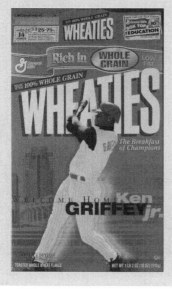

**Ken Griffey Jr. was immortalized on a box of Wheaties cereal in 2000.** (Photo courtesy of Mike Shannon.)

box, as are special accomplishments, such as Pete Rose's setting the all-time record for base hits and Cal Ripken Jr.'s breaking Lou Gehrig's consecutive games played record.

The latest Reds Wheaties box appeared in 2000, and the recipient of the honor was Ken Griffey Jr. Amazingly, it was the first time a player had been honored essentially for being traded! Well, there was a little more to it than that. As the commentary on the back of the box by Cincinnati sportswriter Paul Daugherty indicated, what was being celebrated was Griffey's coming home to the great baseball city where he had grown up as the son of a major league player and where he had played interscholastic ball at Moeller Catholic High School. Also implied in the honor was a pat-on-the-back for Griffey's having taken less money in order to return home and to play for the Reds. Of course, Reds fans are anxiously waiting for the next Reds Wheaties box to appear, which they hope will celebrate the franchise's sixth world championship.

Winning Streak; and a complete run of picture ticket stubs from the final season at Riverfront Stadium.

It certainly helps a Reds collector tremendously if he lives in the Cincinnati area. By doing so, he or she can't help but run into collecting opportunities, even without trying to do so. For instance, anybody who ventured into a Cincinnati post office during the summer of 2001 would have noticed for sale the special envelopes, called "first day covers," celebrating Crosley Field as one of the old ballparks included in the United States Postal Service's tribute to "Baseball's Legendary Playing Fields." The 34¢ Crosley Field stamp was based on a postcard and depicts a night game at the old ballyard. The envelope states that it commemorates the official release of the stamp on June 28, 2001, at the Crosley Field Station, and it features (beside the stamp itself and a special cancellation logo) a beautiful silk cachet aerial depiction of Crosley and the surrounding neighborhood, inside a gold foil border. Inexpensive Reds collectibles—the first day covers cost only $10—don't come any nicer, and this one was easily obtainable all through the summer of 2001 in the Queen City.

The online marketplace has made it easier for Reds fans to find Reds items for sale, no matter where they live. At any given time, several thousand items come up for view on eBay when one searches the Sports Memorabilia, Cards, and Fanshop category. The majority of items are baseball cards, and a certain amount of junk that must be weeded through comes up, too, but a few choice collectibles always seem to be on eBay to tempt most any Reds collector. You can also put the odds in your favor by reading the leading periodical for collectors of sports memorabilia, *Sports Collectors Digest,* as well as the monthly "Reds Collectibles" column in *Reds Report* ("For the Reds Fan Who Needs to Know More"), written by yours truly. A visit to RedsFest is an absolute must for every Reds collector. All the sports memorabilia dealers who set up at the Cincinnati Convention Center for RedsFest highlight whatever Reds items they have, but even if the dealers weren't on hand, RedsFest would still be a golden opportunity for Reds collectors because of the autograph opportunities and the sale of game-used uniforms and equipment by the Reds themselves.

Finally, Reds collections should be considered more than mere accumulations of baseball-related objects. They are connections to personalities and heroes and important events of the past. The Reds have a long and glorious history, and no one knows that better than Reds collectors, for they have the stuff to prove it.

# REDS BLOGS

Although they are routinely ignored and slighted in myriad ways by the powers-that-be, baseball fans are as important to Major League Baseball as anyone else, including the best of the players. The fans, after all, are baseball's customers, and as such they are the ones who foot the bills. If baseball fans ever lose interest in the game, then the game will truly be in trouble. If the American baseball fan weren't so addicted to the game and so loyal and so forgiving, Major League Baseball would already have put itself out of business several times, what with its numerous strikes, squabbles over how to divide up the gargantuan revenue pie, and its countless missteps that reveal an indifference to the needs and desires of the average fan.

One of the distinguishing characteristics of baseball fans, besides their loyalty, is their inventiveness in finding ways to stay ever more personally connected to the game. In addition to the two ways we've already talked about, there is a third method, and the one most recently to have taken root: blogging.

The word "blog" is a shortened form of "web log," and refers to a personal journal maintained in public cyberspace by somebody who wishes for any number of reasons to share his or her thoughts on a particular subject (or on a host of unrelated topics) with the rest of the world. Occasionally, extremely popular blogs can make money by charging for advertising space on the blog, but the vast majority of bloggers run their blogs as a hobby for which they are uncompensated.

You can search for blogs devoted to the Cincinnati Reds by typing "Reds blogs" into Google or Yahoo (or on any other good search engine). Once you find a Reds blog, you can get to a number of the other more popular ones because bloggers invariably provide links to each other. With a little work you can probably also find additional Reds blogs that most of the other Reds bloggers haven't discovered yet or perhaps just haven't linked to yet.

Some of the easier-to-find Reds blogs have pretty straightforward names, such as "Cincinnati Reds Blog." Others try to spice it up a bit: e.g., "Redus and Weep," which is about as clever as you can get with the name for a Reds blog, with its reference to one-time Reds outfielder Gary Redus, who never quite fulfilled his considerable potential. Still others supply subtitles, some of which are helpful in describing the purpose or focus of the blog, some of which are not. For instance, "Cincinnati Reds Blog" says (helpfully) that it is "A day-to-day record of the mind of a Cincinnati Reds fan," while the "Reds (and Blues)" blog provides this vague description: "Reds Baseball for the Well-Rounded Sort." Some of the Reds blogs are pretty vanilla graphically speaking, while others go to more trouble to present a visually interesting site. The "Reds Reporter" blog, for instance, has a wonderful logo: a drawing of a five-o'clock-shadowed TV reporter wearing a fedora while reading the sports report.

Whatever they are named and regardless of the artistry with which they are presented, every Reds blog has the same basic purpose: to provide a forum for the blogger to sound off on the team. And sound off these amateur commentators do! Reds blogs contain a lot of criticism, directed about equally at players not playing well and at the management responsible for those players being on the roster and in the lineup. It is unusual for Reds bloggers to show the restraint of the comment made by D.J., the fan behind the "Reds (and Blues)" blog, after a disastrous Reds visit to Oakland, California, in mid-July 2007: "I'm going to do everyone a small service and not talk about the A's series, okay? Okay." Much more common are all-out harangues that blast mediocre plays and questionable decisions. Implicit in all this criticism is the belief that the blogger could do a better job than the Reds field manager or GM if he or she were only given a chance. Most fans probably suffer the same delusions, and many of them can be heard on sports radio talk shows, stating the obvious ("The Reds need more starting pitching"), repeating what passes as the current prevailing wisdom ("Adam Dunn is not worth a damn because he strikes out too much"), and showing their brilliance by suggesting inane trades that could be made only if the other teams were run by idiots ("We should trade Eric Milton, Alex Gonzalez, and a couple of minor league prospects to the Yankees for Derek Jeter"). The great thing about Reds blogs, for the bloggers at least, is that the blogger doesn't have to worry about being cut off by a radio host and told that his ideas are stupid. The blogger is in complete control and can go on for as long as he likes on any topic. This doesn't mean that the blogger expects everyone to agree with him. Bloggers confident in their own opinions always invite and publish feedback, which can really get a spirited conversation going. Such interaction proves the vitality of the blog.

The best Reds blogs do more than just offer the opinions of the bloggers; they publish game accounts and box scores, which can be archived and retrieved when needed at a later time, and

## REDS WHEATIES BOX CHECKLIST

1937 Ernie Lombardi (small panels with orange background series)
1937 Ernie Lombardi (29 series)
1938 Ernie Lombardi (Biggest Thrills in Baseball series)
1939 Ernie Lombardi (civilian clothes series)
1939 Ernie Lombardi (Personal Pointers series)
1940 Ernie Lombardi (Champs of the U.S.A. series)
1941 Frank McCormick (Champs of the U.S.A. series)
1985 Pete Rose
1989 Johnny Bench, Hall of Fame Induction
1990 Cincinnati Reds, World Championship
2000 Ken Griffey Jr., Welcome Home

they share real information, such as statistics and news, perhaps of a trade or a call-up from the minor leagues. For example, one of the best Reds blogs, a blog called "Red Hot Mama," published a scoop that was obviously thought to be of interest mainly to other females: the marriage of Adam Dunn on November 27, 2006, to "one Rachel Brown." Red Hot Mama named as her source for this juicy tidbit a website that normally has nothing to do with baseball, TheInternetMovieDatabase.com. "Redus and Weep" is as eclectic as any Reds blog, offering as it does a long doggerel poem about the trials and tribulations of GM Wayne Krivsky and former manager Jerry Narron.

Red Hot Mama is like many other Reds bloggers in that she does not state her real name anywhere on her blog, preferring instead to use a pseudonym. Reds bloggers want the world to read their opinions and they revel in having a forum to speak their minds about the Cincinnati Reds, but they also feel a need, it seems, to cling to the privacy of anonymity. It is, after all, easier to criticize than to subject oneself to criticism.

Reds bloggers seem to really enjoy their blogs, almost as much as they love the Reds. If the thought has occurred to you that you might want to start your own Reds blog, you definitely want to check out the leaders in the field first, as follows:

- The Big Red Mechanic
- The Church of Baseball
- Cincinnati Reds Blog
- The Cutting Edge of Cincinnati Reds Commentary
- On Baseball and the Reds
- Red Hot Mama
- Redleg Nation
- Red Reporter
- Reds (and Blues)
- Reds Daily
- Redus and Weep
- We Heart the Reds

## THE ROSIE REDS

The logo is a nifty little red lady wearing a red skirt and a Reds cap on her baseball head, carrying a red baseball bat slung over her red shoulder, and marching off spiritedly, presumably to the ballpark to watch her beloved Reds play ball. The organization is the Rosie Reds, the best team fanclub in the country, and you can see, because of the group's logo, why the common perception is that the Rosie Reds is a ladies-only organization. Not so, says club historian Janet Mueller, who insists that "men have never been excluded from the Rosie Reds." Mueller is also quick to point out that the Rosie Reds recently had a man (Tom Juengling) as their president. "And he did a good job, too," adds Mueller. Mr. Juengling, whose term ran from 2004 to 2006, was the organization's 21st president and its first male president.

If men have never been barred, they haven't exactly joined up in droves, either, probably because the Rosie Reds is predominantly a female organization. The organization's literature states that it was started in June of 1963, "when there was danger of the National League franchise being taken out of Cincinnati." The founding mothers of the Rosie Reds were Jeanette Heinze, Marge Zimmer, Betty Kennedy, and Kate McIntyre, and they decided to do something about the situation. Their contribution to the cause was very sensibly the organizing of like-minded Reds lovers into a club that could do things both to support the team and to encourage others to do the same. The club's mission is stated clearly in the acronym that forms the name of the organization: Rooters Organized to Stimulate Interest and Enthusiasm in the Cincinnati REDS!!!

Notice that no gender preference is stated or implied in this description—as there surely would have been had men started the club. It has to be that name, "Rosie," that causes all the confusion...not to mention the logo. Actually, there are more male Rosie Reds members than one would expect. According to current president Tammy Little, men, many of them husbands of female members, make up about 30 percent of the organization's membership.

In any case, what has never been in doubt is the support that the Rosie Reds receive from the Reds organization itself. The Reds annually donate two free game tickets to each member of the club, send speakers from the front office to the club's preseason luncheon, and promote the club with scoreboard public service announcements during home games that direct fans interested in joining the club to a sign-up booth.

Now that there is no danger of the Reds leaving Cincinnati— if there ever really was—the Rosie Reds have turned their attention toward philanthropic matters. The organization holds a number of raffles and fundraising events, such as a Celebrity Fashion Show (not exactly a big inducement for males to join the organization), which helps the Rosie Reds support the Powell Crosley Jr. Kid Glove Association and endow the scholarships they annually provide to the baseball programs at every one of the colleges and universities in the Cincinnati area. The Rosie Reds are also, make no mistake about it, a social organization. They hold meetings, take tours of Great American Ball Park, make an outing out of a visit to the local racetrack, and attend lots and lots of Reds

# THE HONUS WAGNER OF REDS BASEBALL CARDS

The most famous and most valuable baseball card in the world is the T206 Honus Wagner card, which was included as a giveaway in packs of cigarettes back in the early 1900s when Wagner was still playing for the Pittsburgh Pirates. The card is so valuable because Wagner was one of the all-time greats of baseball and because only a small number of the cards were ever issued. Afraid of influencing children to begin smoking, Wagner asked that his card be withdrawn from the tobacco company's promotion. About 40 of the cards are known to exist, and this scarcity, combined with Wagner's elite status as a player, have made the card the holy grail of baseball card collectors. Top condition samples of the card are probably worth $1 million or more today, and even beat-up versions of the T206 Wagner can fetch bundles of money.

So how valuable is the most valuable Reds card? Well, nothing like the T206 Wagner. The most expensive Reds card would set you back only about $1,000, and that should net you a prime condition 1963 Topps Pete Rose card. The 1963 Rose is that expensive only because it is Rose's rookie card. (As nonsensical as it may seem, a player's rookie card does carry a premium over his subsequent cards; the practice of attaching extra value to rookie cards began sometime in the 1980s.) The value of the 1963 Rose card certainly does not derive from any intrinsic beauty, as the card is really not very attractive. In its 1963 set, Topps included first-year players four-rookies-to-a-card. Rose shares card #537 with Pedro Gonzalez, Ken McMullen, and Al Weis, and all you get of Rose is a tiny photo of his head, sort of a voodoo shrunken-head shot. Much prettier (as baseball cards go) and much cheaper is Rose's second-year card, which even includes a Topps Rookie All-Star team trophy on the front.

When it comes to baseball cards, Pete Rose is no Honus Wagner. Still, $1,000 is nothing to spit at. In fact, it was enough to inspire counterfeit Rose rookie cards, which started appearing after the rookie card craze began. According to Darren Grothaus of The Collectors Connection in

Cincinnati, the counterfeiters were not driven out of business; after settlement in court, they were allowed to re-release the cards after stamping "Counterfeit" on the backs to clearly indicate that the cards were not authentic. Grothaus says that there is a steady demand for the counterfeit Rose rookies, which sell for between $25 and $50.

home games, all in the company of other members. They also make at least one road trip a year, en masse, to support the Reds in hostile territory. And don't get the idea that the Rosie Reds pilgrims are a bunch of decrepit Geritol-sipping geriatrics. No, sir. In fact, according to Little, the Rosie Reds are "party animals...a party waiting to happen!" And there is nothing wrong with that. Remember that the Reds were kicked out of the National League in 1880 because of their refusal to abide by the NL's insistence on ballpark prohibition, and given the organization's total support of the Reds you can understand why the Rosie Reds might occasionally find themselves in a clean, well-lighted tavern or rathskeller, hoisting a toast or two to the team they love. This is not to suggest that the Rosie Reds logo should be altered to depict the red lady weaving unsteadily. Everything in moderation with the Rosie Reds, except for their rooting on the Reds!

# NOTES

Allen, Lee. *The Cincinnati Reds: An Informal History*. New York: G.P. Putnam's Sons, 1948.

Bass, Mike. *Marge Schott: Unleashed*. Champaign, IL: Sagamore Publishing, 1993.

Carney, Gene. *Burying the Black Sox: How Baseball's Cover-Up of the 1919 World Series Fix Almost Succeeded*. Washington, D.C.: Potomac Books, 2006.

Chadwick, Bruce, and David M. Spindel. *The Cincinnati Reds: Memories and Memorabilia of the Big Red Machine*. New York: Abbeville Press, 1994.

*Cincinnati Enquirer*.

*Cincinnati Post*.

Cincinnati Reds Media Guides.

Coberly, Rich. *The No-Hit Hall of Fame: No-Hitters of the 20th Century*. Newport Beach, CA: Triple Play Publications, 1985.

Collett, Ritter. *Men of the Machine*. Dayton, OH: Landfall Press, 1977.

Connor, Floyd, and John Snyder. *Day by Day in Cincinnati Reds History*. New York: Leisure Press, 1983.

Cook, William A. *Pete Rose: Baseball's All-Time Hit King*. Jefferson, NC and London: McFarland & Co., Inc., Publishers, 2004.

Craft, David. "Wheaties: A Hobby Mainstay Celebrates its 75th Anniversary" in *Sports Collectors Digest*. Vol. 26, No. 13 (March 26, 1999), pp. 108–18.

Dellinger, Susan. *Red Legs and Black Sox: Edd Roush and the Untold Story of the 1919 World Series*. Cincinnati: Emmis Books, 2006.

Erardi, John G. *Pete Rose: Baseball's All-Time Hit Leader*. Cincinnati: The Cincinnati Enquirer, 1985.

Gillette, Gary, and Pete Palmer, eds. *The 2006 ESPN Baseball Encyclopedia*. New York: Sterling Publishing Co., 2006.

Gutman, Dan. *Baseball Babylon: From the Black Sox to Pete Rose, the Real Stories behind the Scandals that Rocked the Game*. New York: Penguin, 1992.

Hamilton, Josh, as told to Tim Keown. "I'm Proof that Hope Is Never Lost." *ESPN The Magazine*, Vol. 10, No. 14 (July 16, 2007), pp. 41–47.

Hoard, Greg. *Joe: Rounding Third and Heading Home*. Wilmington, OH: Orange Fraser Press, 2004.

James, Bill. *The Bill James Historical Baseball Abstract*. New York: Villard, 1984.

Libby, Bill. *Johnny Bench: The Little General*. New York, G.P. Putnam's Sons, 1972.

McConnell, Bob, and David Vincent. *SABR Presents the Home Run Encyclopedia: The Who, What, and Where of Every Home Run Hit Since 1876*. New York: Macmillan, 1996.

Pietrusza, David, Matthew Silverman, and Michael Gershman, eds. *Baseball: The Biographical Encyclopedia*. Kingston, NY: Total Sports Illustrated, 2000.

Rathgeber, Bob. *Cincinnati Reds Scrapbook*. Virginia Beach, VA: JCP Corp., 1982.

*Reds Report*.

Rhodes, Greg, and John Erardi. *Big Red Dynasty: How Bob Howsam and Sparky Anderson Built the Big Red Machine*. Cincinnati: Road West Publishing, 1997.

Rhodes, Greg, and John Erardi. *Crosley Field: The Illustrated History of a Classic Ballpark*. Cincinnati: Road West Publishing, 1995.

Rhodes, Greg, and John Erardi. *The First Boys of Summer: The 1869–1870 Cincinnati Red Stockings, Baseball's First Professional Team*. Cincinnati: Road West Publishing, 1994.

Rhodes, Greg, and John Snyder. *Redleg Journal: Year by Year and Day by Day with the Cincinnati Reds Since 1866.* Cincinnati: Road West Publishing, 2000.

Rhodes, Greg, and Mark Stang. *Reds in Black & White: 100 Years of Cincinnati Reds Images.* Cincinnati: Road West Publishing, 1999.

Shannon, Mike. *Johnny Bench.* New York: Chelsea House Publishers, 1990.

Shannon, Mike. *Riverfront Stadium, Home of the Big Red Machine.* Charleston, SC: Arcadia Publishing, 2003.

Skipper, James K. Jr. *Baseball Nicknames: A Dictionary of Origins and Meanings.* Jefferson, NC: McFarland & Co., Inc., 1992.

Stupp, Dann. *Opening Day at Great American Ball Park.* Champaign, IL: Sports Publishing, LLC, 2003.

Vincent, David, Lyle Spatz, and David W. Smith. *The Midsummer Classic: The Complete History of Baseball's All-Star Game.* Lincoln, NE: University of Nebraska Press, 2001.

Wheeler, Lonnie, and John Baskin. *The Cincinnati Game.* Wilmington, OH: Orange Fraser Press, 1988.

Wulf, Steve. "The Big Sweep." *Sports Illustrated*, Vol. 73, No. 18 (October 29, 1990), pp. 18–31.